YOU ME AND EBT

Jahi Kweli

ISBN: 0615570925
ISBN 13: 9780615570921

TABLE OF CONTENTS

Introduction   v

Chapter 1: Before The Swipe   1
Chapter 2: Orientation   7
Chapter 3: From Cerritos to L.A.   15
Chapter 4: Now Hiring   21
Chapter 5: The Big Four   29
Chapter 6: Applications   37
Chapter 7: Resumes   45
Chapter 8: Interviews   59
Chapter 9: Ernie & Luisa   69
Chapter 10: A Warm Cup Of Latte   73
Chapter 11: A refill cup of Hot Latte   85
Chapter 12: It feels like Vegas   91
Chapter 13: The Audacity of His Story   99
Chapter 14: Forever Family   105
Chapter 15: Bring On 2009   113
Chapter 16: Let's Play Job Search   125
Chapter 17: Diamonds in the Rough   135
Chapter 18: Just A Few thoughts   141
Chapter 19: Empowerment   147

INTRODUCTION:

You're driving down a street, and you see a sign hanging in the window of a restaurant, and it reads, "We Accept EBT." How many of us have made an ATM withdrawal and notice the letters "EBT" as a point of sale transaction option? And, of course, we're standing in a grocery store line, we look over at the register, and the forms of payment include: Visa, MasterCard, Discover, American Express, and EBT. I'm sure by now, most of us across the United States of America, the state of California, and in particular, the county of Los Angeles, have grown accustomed to seeing these EBT advertisements on a regular basis. However, many hardworking federal/state taxpayers may not be fully aware of how their public assistance tax dollars are being spent on California's welfare-to-work system. This book will chronicle a period from 1995 to the present while giving you a personal behind the scenes account of how a significant percentage of our able-bodied Los Angeles County welfare-to-work adult recipients are capable of working and earning a legal legitimate living; however, they aren't genuinely, authentically, professionally, and sincerely (GAPS) making an honest job search effort in this highly competitive 21st century job market. Many are not maximizing their full income-earning potential, nor are they effectively marketing themselves. And, despite the quality services my frontline colleagues, including myself, are providing, a growing number of our recipients have become too dependent on the power of the EBT (Electronic Benefit Transfer) card as a normal way of everyday life. California has the friendliest welfare-to-work system nationwide. Are we too welfare friendly? In my own words, observations, and personal/professional opinion-ready, on your marks, get set; let's go!

CHAPTER 1: *Before The Swipe*

First, let's take a look at our federal government's role in establishing, funding, and supporting many programs and services that have affected generations of Americans for over 75 years. Franklin D. Roosevelt's 1933 New Deal Act created temporary relief for the poor/unemployed as a direct result of the 1929 stock market crash that ignited a 25% national unemployment rate. The basic premise of this Act was to reform and stabilize our overall economy. In 1941, Executive Order 8802 prohibited government contractors from participating in unfair hiring practices based on, race, color, or national origin. In 1964, the Civil Rights Act (Title V1) prohibited discrimination based on race, color, and national origin in programs and activities receiving federal financial assistance. In 1963, the Equal Pay Act (EPA) aimed at abolishing wage disparity based on gender. In 1967, Congress passed the Age Discrimination Employment Act (ADEA). The Rehabilitation Act of 1973 prohibited government from discriminating against individuals with disabilities. Seventeen years later, the Title 1 Act of 1990 basically expanded the 1973 Rehabilitation Act.

This leads us to 1996, when former president Bill Clinton signed the Welfare Reform Act. It was the Personal Responsibility Work Opportunity Responsibility Act (PRWORA). Enacted in January of 1997, the name of the block grant that allocates tens of billions of dollars of funds to all of our individual states is called Temporary Assistance For Needy Families (TANF). Notice the key words included in this TANF block grant? "Temporary Assistance," and, not the term permanent assistance. Also note the key words included in PRWORA: Personal Responsibility and Work Opportunity. Therefore, is our federal government encouraging adults receiving public assistance to take personal responsibility for their long-term future by working? Are they suggesting that these legally grown adults take personal responsibility for themselves and their biological offspring by earning a legal legitimate income? In 1997, my home state of California adopted the California Work Opportunity and Responsibility to Kids (CALWORKS). And the key terminology included here is "Work Opportunity" and "Responsibility For Kids."

So is the state of California reminding our CALWORKS recipients in the Golden state that it's their parental responsibility to financially take care of their biological kids via working? Or–once again I dare repeat–earn a legal legitimate income? Think about these questions as we take a closer look behind the scenes of the largest welfare-to-work county program in the U.S.

Here are some general statistics about California and its correlation with welfare recipients: California has approximately 12% of the nation's total population yet 30% of the population on the national welfare roles. It's estimated that there are about 1.5 million people receiving hundreds of millions of dollars in state/federal funds. Overall, the state/federal government has done its part in establishing legislation aimed at assisting economically disadvantaged U.S. citizens, with the intent on improving the quality of life for all Americans. Inspired by 18 years of experience on the "front line" of California's welfare-work system, I felt compelled to share this story with those of you hard-working taxpayers, who are funding our programs via your tax dollars to provide a first-hand, behind the scenes account of Los Angeles County's welfare-to-work programs.

Here's a story some of you may not have heard about. The *Los Angeles Times* reported that in June of 2010, $12k was recuperated from 17 different gentleman's strip clubs/casinos in Los Angeles county from ATM machines that honored the EBT cash transactions. Lizelda Lopez, spokeswoman for the Department of Public Social Services e-mailed the L.A. Times staff, assuring that future EBT cash transactions have been deactivated at those aforementioned locations. I'm not sure how many of you hard-working taxpayers realized that a portion of your hard-earned tax dollars are paying the bill for gambling and lap dances. Subsequently, the 10-5-10 Los Angeles Times follow-up report entitled, "Making It Rain On Welfare" revealed that a segment of California welfare recipients spent $69 million on "living the good life." Here's a breakdown on how our hard-earned taxpayer dollars were spent: Las Vegas: $11 million–which included gambling, shopping, and hotel stay. Approximately $1.5 million were spent on cruise ships, which included destinations like Miami, Rio de Janeiro, Florida, and the Hawaiian Islands. Attention all taxpayers funding California's EBT benefits! Do I have your attention yet? OK, so fasten your seat-belts as we take a closer look at how a significant percentage of Los Angeles county welfare-to-work recipients aren't making a genuine, authentic, professional, and sincere (GAPS) effort regarding their job searches.

My journey serving on the front line in Los Angeles County's welfare-to-work began in February of 1993. As an Employment Advisor with the Los Angeles Urban League, I provided pre-employment training, job development assistance, and job placement services to adults receiving public assistance. Their barriers/challenges to obtaining gainful employment consisted of substance abuse, mental health, homelessness, illiteracy, and felony convictions. In 1995, I joined the Los Angeles County office of Education (LACOE) as a Career Development Program Specialist (formerly known as a Job Search Specialist), providing the same services we provided during my tenure with the L.A. Urban League. LACOE has been providing Job Skills Preparation Classes to adult welfare recipients in Los Angeles County since the inception of the Greater Avenues for Independence (GAIN) division back in 1993. LACOE has an impressive resume regarding strong leadership: the LACOE board of supervisors; three retired and very well respected former superintendents; a current superintendent who is continuing the tradition of professionalism, service, and embracing multicultural diversity; two greatly admired former GAIN division directors; and a current GAIN division director who's all of the aforementioned and just an all-around awesome guy.

My fellow Career Development Program Specialists (CDPS) for LACOE are absolutely incredible job coaches. They bring impeccable higher education degrees to the table, compassion, expertise, and a wealth of experience to the front line of the largest welfare-to-work county nationwide, they are truly the BEST. I would be remiss if I didn't acknowledge our clerical/administrative team, Career Development Program Assistants, and office Assistants. They are undoubtedly the heart and soul of our division and vital to the day-to-day operations of each site. Words cannot begin to describe the overall respect I have for my frontline staff colleagues. An adult that enters any of the many Department of Public Social Services (DPSS) offices in Los Angeles County, and requests financial public assistance, must meet minimum state/federal eligibility requirements, which is not limited to but includes such things as: age, citizenship, housing status, and financial hardship. Eligibility is determined by an assigned Eligibility Worker (EW) via a very thorough intake eligibility process. Once the applicant is determined eligible to receive these state/federal public assistance funds, and they have gone through a very detailed process, which also evaluates their employability status, they become clients. Clients who are deemed unemployable are exempted from participating in a Job Skills Preparation Component (JSPC) and must be referred to designated evaluators such as: the Department of Rehabilitation; County Mental Health; and an medical evaluation to determine legitimacy of unemployables status. 100% of all those clients who are referred to the Job Skills Preparation Component class are deemed employable. Let me REPEAT this one more time so everyone understands me loud and clear: 100% of all those clients who are referred to the Job Skills Preparation Component class are deemed EMPLOYABLE! What does this mean? It means that they are capable of working/earning a legal/legitimate living.

I must take a moment to give my respects to the EWs who are outstanding! They carry case-loads of low-high hundreds each and every month, while providing quality services in approving the client's benefits. The clients who are assigned to the Orientation Motivation Component become Participants (PTs); the PTs are then assigned to a GAIN/Grow Services Worker (GSW), who will assign/enroll them into JSPC classes, unless PTs qualify for a one semester vocational/college exemption, or a mental or physical exemption that prohibits them from obtaining employment/earning a legal/legitimate living. GSWs do an awesome job managing case-loads, and assigning PTs into various program components.

In the Orientation Motivation classes we provide our PTs with general information such as purpose of these classes, electronic benefit transfer (EBT card) approval process, mental health, substance abuse, domestic violence, and homeless court benefits (where up to thousands of dollars of unpaid citations are fully dismissed-compliments of taxpayer dollars), services, one semester of vocational training/ higher education Job Skills Preparation class exemption, complimentary internet access (compliments of taxpayer dollars) for job search purposes, fax/copy machine usage, and additional services in order to help support them in their transitioning into the job market.

We also inform them about the various Jobs Skills Component classes, where we instruct the PTs on: completion of job applications, resume formats, interview techniques, job development assistance/strategies, breaking down barriers/challenges to obtaining employment, and additional workshops designed to equip our PTs with invaluable job search strategies, and ultimately obtain employment.

CHAPTER 2: *Orientation*

Our Orientation classes are both informational and participatory–make no mistake about it, we are the largest county providing quality welfare-to-work services nationwide. Our geographical jurisdiction includes 17 sites, covering the entire Los Angeles County areas from the northern part of Palmdale/Lancaster, to the eastern border of Pomona, to the city of Carson, and throughout the various cities in Los Angeles, California. As a CDPS facilitator for the LACOE GAIN Division, we're sub-contracted under the Los Angeles County DPSS (with the largest welfare caseloads, statewide/nationwide) to provide these professionally facilitated orientation motivation sessions and job skills preparation classes that lead to job placement. Once the doors of the orientation classes shut and the sessions begin, one would have to sit-in and witness first-hand the various challenges/barriers many of our participants face in obtaining gainful employment. A large percentage of our PTs face barriers such as transitional living, substance abuse, mental health, illiteracy, basic education (no high school diploma/GED), victims of domestic violence, child-support injunctions, product of foster care system, grooming/hygiene deficiencies, felony record convictions. All of these are legitimate barriers to employment; however, they're still able and/or capable of earning a legal/legitimate living.

Think about how many of your co-workers/colleagues and family members are facing similar or identical barriers and challenges to earning a legal legitimate income that our PT'S face regarding obtaining jobs/careers in our various respective professions. How did they get their jobs? What's driving them to keep their jobs? Even with such a sluggish economy, with an almost double-digit nation-wide unemployment rate, people are still obtaining employment. What are the inside trade secrets to their employment success? And, with many Americans in the work-force experiencing similar barriers to employment that our PTs face, how are they still able and/or capable of earning a legal/legitimate living? Think about these questions as we move forward in taking a closer look behind the scenes of L.A. County's welfare-to-work program.

Unfortunately, over the years I've been observing a significant percentage of our PTs take a spiraling downward turn into not making a GAPS employment search effort, in spite of all the support they've been given. The first portion of the Orientation session consists of testing the PTs' reading and writing competency levels. Next, we provide them with general information regarding the many services available to them. Finally, we inform them about rules, regulations, and expectations of the Job Skills Preparation Classes. There are so many stories to share about the daily activities that take place in our orientation sessions that would literally shock most people outside of our profession, so I'll share just a few stories that may enlighten you on the daily challenges we face in preparing this population in entering/re-entering the job market. Also, keep in mind that by the time a Participant completes our orientation sessions, 100% of them are deemed employable…

These are true stories, using fictitious names to protect true identities of the PTs. Generally, when I facilitate orientation or JSPC classes, I've adopted two personality traits that enable me to effectively conduct the facilitation of these classes while maintaining my professional sanity. When it comes to my facilitation style, I have received many flattering written remarks conveying my professionalism, respectfulness, knowledgeable, patience, expertise, and motivation/inspiration, with a little touch of humor. These are the words that have come from literally thousands of evaluation forms submitted by our PTs over the years expressing their appreciation for the experience they had with me as their facilitator. I'll call this personality trait "Mr. President" (MP) for illustration purposes. Now my other personality trait is my ultimate filtration system. He filters out ALL non-sense, bull-shit, mean-spiritedness, know-it-alls, dumb-asses, wise-asses, and much more toxic waste from PTs who display that type of unprofessional behavior. Let's call him "Fool Please" (FP). Orientation begins with the welcoming/house-keeping rules which include no eating, no sleeping/heads down, no cell phone usage, no smoking cigarettes, no smoking marijuana, no alcoholic beverages, no verbally threatening/offensive language, no excessive ins and outs of classroom etc. With all this said, here are some examples of the daily challenges we face in many of our orientation classes.

Now, I must give you a little insight about what goes on in my mind seconds before I verbally respond to challenging situations that go on in these classes. There are frequent split-second conversations I have in my mind between MP and FP. It's a morning orientation class, we've just finished the general questionnaire, and as I look over to my left at the very end of the front row, I notice one of our PTs rolling up what appeared to my naked eye as a marijuana joint (weed, chronic, ganja, blunts, spliffs, ooh wee sticky icky, etc.) MP asked him, "Sir! What is that you're rolling up right before my eyes in the front row?"

Sticky Icky Ricky looked up at me with an extremely nonchalant response, "What? It's just tobacco."

MP responded, "Look Sticky Icky Ricky, it looks like weed, and even if it's just tobacco, we just went over the house-keeping rules where I clearly stated no cigarettes/marijuana allowed in these classrooms period!"

Sticky Ricky replied, "You just said we can't smoke it. You didn't say anything about rolling it up!"

An immediate response from FP to MP: *Now I know this weed rolling, dope-dealing, captain roll-em-up fool doesn't think we're gonna support his street pharmaceutical sales profession up in here?* "Ain't no puff-puff-pass up in here fool!" MP informed him to take that stuff out of the classroom.

"Ooh wee," Sticky Icky Ricky replied, "so what, ya'll just gone kick-me-out?"

MP says, "Yes, sir, you're immediately dismissed."

While this situation was going on, in the same class I had two simultaneous situations that needed my immediate attention. One of our PTs was sleeping in the back right corner, while another one was on his phone excessively texting in one of the front middle seats. At first, I made another general class announcement reminding everyone about the no sleeping/text-ting policy in class. Not 10 damn minutes from me reminding everyone, Tommy Text-Master and Peter Power Nap continued to engage in their respectively and blatantly disrespectful violation of the class rules. At that point, I called out both names and gave them ultimatums to immediately stop text-ting/sleeping, or face dismissal from orientation.

Wonder what happened next? Well, Tommy Text-Master responded by saying, "I can hear you. I ain't gotta look at you." Peter Power Nap rolled his evil eyes at me and went right back to sleep. Yes he did folks! FP could barely be contained and began shouting in my ear, *Oh hell nah! No, Tommy Text-Master did not just say what I thought he said? And, Peter Power Nap is rolling his evil eyes at me!* First, I had Tommy Text-Master repeat his response to me one more time just for clarity's sake and to make sure I heard him correctly. Yep! His punk ass repeated, "I said, I can hear you. I ain't gotta look at you. You handle yours and I'll handle mine." Needless to say, both Tommy Text-Master and Peter Power Nap were immediately escorted out of the building by county police. Here is a list of other every-day challenges that go on in many of our daily orientation classes: strong weed/marijuana, alcohol beverage aromas, horrible body odors, mental health disorder break-downs, substance abuse withdrawals (tweaking), stone-faced severe illiteracy, bi-polarism, non-participation, etc. Everyone has a story right? And, the population groups receiving these EBT benefits are getting younger and younger.

First and foremost, there is an alarming growing trend of 18-24 year-olds participating in our programs. With this young population, I always encourage them to finish their General Education Diploma's (GED's) (if they never received a high school diploma) and enroll in community college, trade school, vocational training, or various other certification courses. One of our young PTs informed the class that his grandma, two aunts, and his mother are ALL receiving EBT benefits. When I asked him if any of them are encouraging him to finish his GED and pursue higher educational/vocational training, he responded, "Nah, they ain't tripping on that. They just wanted me to get these benefits." We remind them that every community has an adult school, vocational school, community college, or church that offers a GED program. It's up to these young folks to take advantage of these state/federally funded programs. Often times, we discover that their home environments don't foster, don't encourage, and don't support the youth's educational success. They come from homes that have challenges such as generational welfare, substance abuse, mental health, gang-violence, high school drop-outs, domestic violence, victims of sexual assault/molestation, incarceration, etc. As a staff we do our very best to encourage, support, and instill motivation in them so that they may achieve tremendous success in their future endeavors.

Overall, the county offers services that will begin the process of addressing these challenges/barriers; however, we are fighting against so many negative non-supportive forces in their lives that it becomes an extremely difficult cycle to break. We regularly get youth who currently/previously have/had gang-affiliations. Most of their gang-involvement includes drug sales, criminal activities, or youth/adult incarceration. Many are afraid to separate from their gang lives due to various retaliatory consequences. A small percentage of our youth come from healthier home/neighborhood environments where they've become comfortable with receiving government benefits and they fear growing up and accepting adult responsibilities of earning a legal/legitimate living. When we share with them the advantages of working versus not working, some are inspired and some aren't. One of our young impressionable PTs, Hustle-Man, straight forwardly asked me in a morning Orientation class, "Jahi, why should I work when I can make more money out there hustling on the streets than I could flipping burgers or stacking boxes? And, I'm living in a three-bedroom, two-bath-section 8 property home, in a million dollar community overlooking the entire beach coastal areas? I go into my bedroom, plop down on my black La-Z-Boy recliner, admire my exotic fish tank aquarium, turn on my 55-inch plasma television, watch my sports programs, smoke some weed, and chill. When I want some lovin'/romance, I knock on my girl's door down-the-hall! Why should I work, Dawg?"

I responded by congratulating him on his current lap of luxury living on taxpayers' expenses. However, I asked him what would happen if he ever broke up with his live-in girlfriend? What happens when the time limits of her section 8 living runs out? What would you do then? I also questioned his alleged successful street hustling skills by asking, "First of all, if you're street hustling skills are all that, why are you here? Secondly, your street hustling skills must not be good because you're swiping an EBT card with a maximum of $421 dollars a month. You can flip burgers and stack boxes for at least $450 dollars a month working part-time."

His response was, "I ain't gonna work that hard. I'm just here to get this free County money."

I further elaborated my answer to Hustle-Man's question by saying, "Also, one day all of those illegal street hustling activities will get you a pre-mature casket in the grave, incarceration, and/or spending your latter adult/senior citizen years swiping an EBT card." In my classes I share a plethora of true stories that are intended to provide examples of how not to make the same mistakes others before them have made. So I shared a short story with Hustle-Man about some of the negative consequences that often happen when people involve themselves in illegal street activities.

During my teenage years growing up in Gardena, California, most of my friends began to understand and realize the value of having money and how it affects everyday living. When I was 16 years old, my mother encouraged me to get a job at our local neighborhood gas station. I worked some very challenging part-time hours after school pumping gas, checking/refilling fluids, checking tire pressure, changing tires, wiping windows, spot-sweeping/emptying garbage, degreasing mechanics' work-stations, purchasing automotive products, and sanitizing restrooms. That experience gave me tremendous motivation to go to college and earn a degree. Unfortunately, one of my close childhood friends, Little Bo, decided to become an illegal street pharmaceutical representative (drug dealer). Now, as he began to floss brand new clothes, top-of-the-line shoe gear, gold/diamond jewelry, money clips filled with $100 dollar bills, and new cars every week, I must admit that I was very tempted to get a little taste of the action. However, the basic lessons of right and wrong, and the value of legal legitimate work ethics taught by my mother prevented me from getting involved in the narcotics game. As I graduated from high school with high honors, I embarked upon a college career that laid the foundation of my current profession in social services. Little Bo ended up serving 13 years in state prisons as a result of his drug sales involvement.

After almost 20 years of our lives taking on contrasting directions, I ran into him a few years back at one of our favorite neighborhood parks. When we spotted one another, it was like old times. We immediately embraced each other and began to share our stories about what each one had been up to all those years. Little Bo had a whole lot to share about how his life took a crazy turn for the worst. Along with serving the 13 years in prison, he lost everything. The government seized his properties, cars, liquidated/auctioned various purchased items, and froze/closed bank accounts. Not a few weeks later, he enrolled into one of our orientation classes, and guess who was his facilitator? Yep, it was me! Talk about life's unexpected moments, huh? After class, we had a long discussion about moving forward in a positive manner. I also asked him what gave him the motivation/inspiration to change his life and move forward in a positive direction. He replied simply, "My daughter! I gotta be there to help raise her! And I wanna make sure she knows that I'm in her life for good now, and that I'll never leave her alone again." My childhood friend Little Bo ended up getting hired at the same local neighborhood gas station I worked at in Gardena, CA when I was 16 years old. Talk about life's full circles moments, huh? The pay was a long way from the high six figure drug money income lifestyle he was accustomed to making; however, the financial sacrifice he made to be in his daughter's life was worth more than what the drug money lifestyle could ever afford him. He realized that no one could put a price tag on that! Hustle-Man's response to this story was, "Well Ya boy got caught slippin, that ain't gonna happen to me."

Sadly, over the years we've lost several of our PT youth to gang violence, domestic violence, the drug game, and incarceration. Too many lives lost before they could ever realize their ultimate true potential on this earth. If they only had one positive family member to lead them in the right direction, maybe there would have been different outcomes. That's why I feel we should continue funding community youth programs that foster a healthier/positive environment such as the Boys & Girls Club, YMCA/YWCA, after school programs, city parks and recreation programs, etc. There are way too many youth who are being raised in deplorably unhealthy living environments.

Now, once a PT completes the Orientation session, they are scheduled for one of our other component class choices. There is the three-week JSPC, in which we cover completion of applications, resume formats, interview techniques, goal-setting, job search/development strategies, and individual/group motivational activities. The four-week

Fastrak class is primarily designed for the older PT who has gone through JSPC previously; however, they still remain unemployed. These workshops are specifically designed for their individual needs to break down barriers to employment such as mental, emotional, ethnic, or age discrimination in intense one-one sessions or additional workshops that would address their needs. The six-week Rapid Employment Program (REP) is for those PTs who have recent work experience, or acceptable pre-employment skills/abilities—overall, limited barriers to employment; however, due to the state of our current economy, their unemployment benefits have run out and they're temporarily utilizing government funds while continuing their job search. REP PTs have the same accommodations as the JSPC/Fastrak PTs. They all have access to fax machines, internet, phone usage, job lead/development, and overall one-on-one support in their job search progress.

When I first began facilitating these JSPC classes back in 1995 for LACOE, I must admit the job market was totally different. Most companies didn't conduct criminal background checks or drug tests; obtaining employment wasn't nearly as challenging and competitive as it is now. One year prior, back in 1994, I had just completed a year as a Vocational Skills Facilitator for Social Vocational Services (SVS) in Irwindale, California, which was funded by the Department of Rehabilitation. And the population we provided job placement services for were high functioning developmentally challenged adults diagnosed with various conditions such as manic depression, schizophrenia, Down syndrome, muscular-related degenerative diseases, etc. One thing I greatly admired about this developmentally challenged adult population is that they didn't allow their conditions/barriers to prevent them from working.

CHAPTER 3: *From Cerritos to L.A.*

My first site assignment for LACOE back in March of 1995 was the Cerritos Greater Avenues for Independence (GAIN) site. Our GAIN division has been sub-contracted under DPSS to provide quality pre-employment job services to GAIN PTs since 1993. Since 1998 LACOE-GAIN has been sub-contracted under DPSS to provide the same quality services to the General Relief (GR) population. Professionals outside of our industry often ask us what the differences are between both GAIN and GR PTs. I often respond by replying "NOT MUCH!" The maximum funds GAIN PTs receive on their EBT cards are generally higher due to parental custodial obligation responsibilities, the content of the workshops differ slightly, and the GR population is deemed harder to serve or with more challenges/obstacles in obtaining gainful employment.

Let's go back in time once again. It's March of 1995. I walk into the International Brotherhood of Electrical Workers (IBEW) building in Cerritos where my LACOE career began facilitating JSPC workshops. I was warmly greeted by a few senior colleagues who quickly embraced me as one of their teammates. The first week at our Cerritos site consisted of daily classroom observations of JSPC curriculum presentation, paperwork procedures, site rules/regulations, local eateries, overall day-day operations of the site. As I was observing the first day of JSPC class, the instructor went around the room and had all 20 PTs introduce themselves and share with the class why they made the decision to apply for public assistance. What events happened in their lives that led them to become participants in our class? The gender make-up of the class consisted of majority women, and there were two men. None of them had any major barriers to employment. Some wanted to finish their GEDs, attend college, vocational training, or additional certification programs in various industries. There were a few women who dealt with domestic violence issues, some married as young teenagers, and then later faced separation/divorce; others faced minor employment challenges which were subsequently addressed during the five-day JSPC sessions. Emotions ran high as these women began discussing what gave them motivation/inspiration to transition off public assistance: their children. That was inspiring for me to hear that because I knew then and I still know to this day that most women who truly LOVE their children want the very best for them. By the end of that three-week class, over 50% of those ladies obtained gainful employment, and several other ladies began vocational training classes; just a handful including the two men ended up self-dropping out due to personal decisions.

The first class I facilitated garnered a 48% job placement and a few self-drops; the remainder attended vocational training and opted to complete their GED's. The most striking thing that really stood out during my first month at this site was the amazing Positive Mental Attitude (PMA) of the PTs. We hardly ever had a negative PT. It was a breath of fresh air facilitating those classes because of their incredible positive outlook on the possibilities of their futures. I remember telling all of my family/friends that I couldn't understand how many of our L.A. county welfare-to-work recipients were getting a bad rap with many negative accusations. Subsequently, I finished the 1994-1995 fourth quarter fiscal year at 48% job placement with a small percentage of drops; the remaining were positive completions. By the end of the first quarter of the 1995-1996 fiscal year, my job placement percentages increased to 55%.

At the end of the 2nd quarter of the 1995-1996 fiscal year, my job placement percentages ballooned to 65%! Things were going extremely well. I was literally on cloud nine when I walked through those IBEW doors because I truly felt that we had a WINNING system that was working–soaring job placements, very low drops, positive completions, exceptional positive mental attitudes among the PT's, and an amazing team spirit relationship with my colleagues. Well, that changed when our senior/middle-management decided to shake things up and transfer staff to different sites. So I received the official involuntary administrative transfer to one of our downtown L.A. sites.

Its holiday season late December 1995, and I entered the downtown L.A. site parking lot still singing, "Chestnuts roasting on an open fire..." As I parked my car, and then exited the vehicle, I was greeted by the parking lot attendants and I informed them that I was a new transfer staff from LACOE, and if they could direct me to the GAIN office. So, one of their attendants escorted me inside the building where I was received by one of my senior colleagues. Once inside the building, the site supervisor greeted me with a warm welcome, and for the next couple of hours, I was given staff introductions, a tour of the building facilities, paper-work procedures, rules/regulations, and the overall style of the site. Throughout the morning, Christmas music was playing and everyone appeared to be in great holiday spirits. Next, our site supervisor informed me that I would be facilitating the afternoon JSPC class. I responded with GREAT enthusiasm. I couldn't wait to transfer the same winning system from Cerritos over to Downtown L.A. She looked at me with a surprised facial expression and responded, "Nice to see your excitement. Everything's set-up in the classroom, so if you need our help/assistance just let us know." Inside I was thinking, *I don't need any help this will be a piece of cake, no problem right?* WRONG! Little did I know that the dark clouds were about to rain on my cheerful sunshine parade very shortly thereafter.

Lunchtime was nice. I strolled down the street to a Greek eatery restaurant and ordered my favorite vegetarian falafel plate. As I re-entered the building early to prepare for my afternoon class, I set-up the classroom materials/visual aids according to my normal facilitation format routine. I then returned to my desk to get into what I call "pre-game" mind-set. Right on cue, I turned on the radio and heard Donny Hathaway's "This Christmas" playing. Filled with holiday spirit joy, I was damn near skipping to the classroom, as the 1pm hour approached. Humming "This Christmas," I entered into a max capacity filled room of 40 PTs awaiting the start of class. Before I approached the front of the class, one PT shouted out, "It's about damn time you came—you our teacher?" Another PT was snoring and sleeping on the left-side front row, one young lady had on a combination see through skirt/blouse outfit that exposed everything. It looked like a handkerchief was covering her breasts and a dinner napkin was around her waist. Girlfriend might as well have been butt-naked! She left absolutely nothing to the imagination. I introduced myself to the class as their instructor for the next three weeks, or until they became employed.

Not a second after that introduction, the very first question was, "Ya'll gone get us jobs?"

I responded by repeating, "We will assist you in obtaining gainful employment, yes."

Another interrupted by asking me, "What does 'gainful employment' mean?"

I replied, "We'll assist you in getting a job."

The same person who blurted out "ya'll gone get us jobs" once again blurted out, "I don't know about gainful employment, but I know ya'll 'posed to get us jobs, immediately!"

There was a brief conversation between MP and FP. MP began assessing this new environment and concluded that FP needed to handle this situation. FP told MP *Step aside DAWG! I got this 'because this girl's tripping!* FP asked the lady, "What part of 'we're going to help you guys get jobs/obtain gainful employment' don't you understand? Come on now young lady, for real!" As I had each PT introduce him/her-self to the class, we followed each introduction with a fun applause such as We Will Rock You (Queen's-sports anthem), Wazup from Martin Lawrence show, or The Addams Family theme song.

Of course, Lady Big Mouth had to put in her two cents before it was her turn. She blurted out, "This shit's childish! I didn't come here for this!"

FP responded, "Then leave! You're excused! No one is forcing you to stay here!" So she got up and excused herself. Mind you, we were only into the first 30 frickin' minutes of day one of a three-week JSPC class. I knew I was in for a long three weeks.

Now, the PT who was snoring at the beginning of class Sir-Snore-a-lot was given two polite warnings during the introductions "No sleeping in class!" One would think that two very polite/professional reminders about the no sleeping and snoring in class policy would do the trick right? Wrong! Ole Sir-Snore-a-lot decided to give me the evil eye; then rolled his eyes, smacked his lips and said, "I ain't bothering nobody."

FP responded, "Yeah, you are–you're bothering me! So, you either both stay awake and participate in this class or you can excuse yourself."

He replied, "You ain't saying nut tin anyway," and excused himself.

My third situation came from an alleged gang-banger who kept talking to his female neighbor during the introductions. I made another general class announcement reminding everyone to show one another courtesy/respect while someone's talking. As we continued class introductions, Mr. Thug Life totally ignored my request and continued talking with the young lady. At that point, I singled him out. His name tent referenced a common gang-affiliated name and I called him by that name and gave him a FINAL WARNING to cease with the out-of-turn, rude sidebar conversations or face immediate dismissal. Thug-Life responded by saying, "Man Cuzz," (Crip language), "don't talk to me like a child! This shit's for kids Cuzz."

FP replied, "You know what? You're excused!" Thug-Life abruptly got up and aggressively walked towards my direction, as if he was going to who bang on me, (gangster language for "get in my face"). I immediately went into my martial arts self-defense position. As he approached my direction with a mean snarly facial expression, I watched him angrily shove/slam the door open, while using inappropriate profanity. Upon taking a few inhale/exhale pauses, I apologized to the remaining class for the unprofessional/rude behavior exhibited by those three individuals. Nevertheless, we concluded the introductions, paper-work, and remaining day one JSPC activities.

Later that evening, I remember having a long conversation with my mother explaining the details of a rough first day at the new site. She supported my actions and encouraged me to hang in there. I made a promise to myself on that night, and to this day I follow it to a tee. I said, "From this point forward, I will always allow MP to set the table; however, FP will always be locked, loaded and ready to fire away when needed, at the drop of a hat." The egregious negative attitudes will not be tolerated in my classes! Taxpayer's dollars are funding these programs in hopes that ALL of our welfare-to-work participants will transition off of the welfare rolls. Negative attitudes from ungrateful, unappreciative, disrespectful, mean-spirited, classless, and unprofessional PTs should not, and will not, be tolerated!

This invaluable technique has enabled me to maintain my professional composure over the years, while providing quality facilitation services to our JSPC workshops. At the end of this class's three-week period, there were 35 enters, 20 drops, 4 jobs, 11 completes with no job. Needless to say, I wasn't pleased with the overall stats of my first class at the new site. As the last PT was exiting our office on the last day of JSPC with a certificate of completion in her hand, she noticed I was feeling a little dejected about the final results of this class experience. She verbally praised me as the best instructor/teacher she ever had, including a couple of college courses. With great appreciation I thanked her for those warm compliments. She gave me a professional encouragement hug and told me to keep doing what I was doing because I was an excellent instructor. As I read my first 20 evaluations from the PTs, I received excellent evaluations overall. The ratings went from 1=lowest, 2=needs much improvement, 3=average/ok, 4=good, 5=Excellent. Twelve of the 20 had rated me excellent overall, six gave me half excellent, half good marks, and only two PTs gave me a combination of one and two. Upon discovering that my fellow site colleagues were dealing with the same challenges, and that the overall site job placement percentage averaged around 15%. That was the defining moment where I realized that I wasn't the crazy one. These PTs needed to step up to the ground level of basic job searching strategies/techniques. From that moment, I wouldn't second guess nor doubt my teaching STYLE!

CHAPTER 4: *Now Hiring*

From 1995-2000, there have been so many employers that have jumped on and then off the bandwagon of hiring welfare-to-work PTs at our various L.A. county sites that it's almost embarrassing. One day back in early 1998 I had a long discussion with a recruitment manager named Alex from one of the largest leading staffing agencies in Los Angeles County. He shared with me story after story about the many challenges most of his frontline recruiters were having with the majority of their welfare-to-work case-loads. Alex said about 25% of them don't even show up for the first day of the assignment. 50% that do show up don't even complete the very first week, and only about 10% actually complete the full term of their respective assignments. When he proceeded to tell me the reasons/excuses they came up with, I shook my head in disbelief! Here are some of the reasons/excuses for those who didn't show up for the first day of the assignment:

1. Couldn't find the place, so they just went back home.
2. Fell asleep on the bus woke up too late to go to work.
3. Missed the bus.
4. Had real bad diarrhea.
5. Couldn't get a ride to/from worksite.
6. Wanted an assignment closer to their house.
7. Got arrested the night before.
8. Got into a fight with their significant other.
9. Stuck in Tijuana, Mexico.
10. No one told them they were supposed start on assignment day.
11. Wanted a little more pay.
12. The cops came and sectioned off our street so no one was allowed to leave.
13. Can't go in that area 'cause that's one of my rival gang territories.
14. Cramping, PMS.
15. Hangover from the night before.

16. Overslept.
17. Didn't want that job to affect my EBT benefits.
18. I had something to do, but can I go the next day?

Now, here are some reasons why those PTs resigned before the end of the first week:

1. The company worked them too hard.
2. They didn't get enough smoke breaks.
3. Supervisor didn't allow staff's significant others at workstation areas.
4. They were racist.
5. The staff didn't like the PT.
6. PT didn't get along with my supervisor. (The first frickin week on the job?)
7. PT needed a day off and management wouldn't give it to me. (Once again, the first frickin week?).
8. Didn't like micro-managing by supervisors.
9. I was sleeping in the break room.
10. I just can't work all those hours.

Needless to say, Alex and his staffing agency jumped off the welfare-to-work bandwagon citing irreconcilable differences between this population and his agency. Remember, this was back in the hey-day of jobs aplenty during the Clinton administration. He told me flat out, "Jahi, it makes no good business sense to continue working with the majority of this population when we've had so many problems; they're flat-out embarrassing to us and the employer who is paying us to pre-screen professionally qualified staff." I understood his company's position and our professional relationship with that agency dissipated quite rapidly. There are countless other agencies/employers that, at some point or another, severed ties with our organization due to the unfortunate unprofessional misconduct by many of our PTs.

During the summer of 1998, my college roommate and current life-long friend called me one day about some exciting news about offering employment opportunities to our PT's. Allow me to set the table... At the time, my good buddy Luke was District Manager of one of the biggest soft drink beverage bottling company's worldwide—with a huge domestic and international global market share. Well, he informed me that all of his regional senior vice presidents wanted to- jump-on this welfare-to-work band-wagon in a BIG way. I said, "Cool! What's the game-plan?" He said their goal was to hire between 200-250 PTs during the 1998/1999 fiscal year. I said, "What!" This truly was going to be an incredible opportunity for many of our PTs to obtain jobs/careers with a solid reputable domestically/internationally growing global company that offers: great pay, benefits, 401k, etc. Before getting off the phone with my friend, I enthusiastically assured him that we would send them the cream-of-the-crop PTs for the initial first round of interviews. That same day, I immediately informed my fellow colleagues/ site supervisor of this incredible opportunity of a lifetime for our PTs. We circulated a memo to the surrounding sites in order to recruit, the top-of-the-line, best-of-the-best, and cream-of-the crop applicants for these interviews. Mind you, many companies didn't aggressively start doing mandatory drug-test/criminal back-ground checks until around 2000. We, on the other hand, took no chances.

The requirements they needed to participate in our prep-session were: must have at least one to two years of recent retail, sales, customer service and/or driving experience; no felony convictions or questionable misdemeanors such as petty theft; be able to pass the drug test. We received an overwhelming response during the first few days of advertising this beverage bottling company recruitment announcement. So, my colleagues and I sifted/sorted through applications/resumes ensuring we would only prepare the best-of-the-best. We invited around 40 applicants to participate in an extremely thorough prep session where we totally prepared them for the first round of interviews. The prep-session consisted of effective application writing, targeting resumes to match this company's profile, powerful interview strategies/techniques, informational research about the company and their rich history, one-on-one review of applications, and final mock interview critiques. Overall, we prepared them as if they were being interviewed by the company CEO himself. Upon the completion of this two-day workshop preparation, my colleagues and I felt very confident that the first interview round would go exceptionally well. We faxed over all of the 40 resumes to my friend Luke before the end of that week, and he and his colleagues scheduled 25 interviews for that following Monday morning. My co-workers and I were elated to say the very least. We immediately called the first 25 selected for the Monday morning interviews and wished them best of luck.

That weekend I remember hanging out with Luke excited about our new partnership with one of leading beverage companies globally. As I headed back home, I couldn't stop smiling about the possibilities that this new partnership could potentially produce… Monday morning couldn't have gotten there fast enough (Or could it have?). Finally, it's Monday morning. As I was driving in to work, I remember looking up at the beautiful sunny southern California skies and thinking, *this is the Big Day!* While over on the other side of town in Orange County, CA, Luke and his senior bosses, which included the Senior District Manager and Regional VP, walked into the main lobby, where our 25 PTs were seated awaiting the start of the interview process. What happened next should only have been seen on the Carol Burnett Show, SNL, MADD TV, In Living Color, or maybe The Dave Chappelle show, but never, never, ever in a professional job interview setting. Luke later told me via phone that they cancelled the remaining interviews as a result of the following circus like scene. The moment Luke and his colleagues first approached the lobby, one of our PTs kept pacing to/from her chair to the front desk receptionist complaining, "How much longer this thang gone take? They got us waiting out here too long." Another lady exposed her hairy unshaved legs with a dress that looked like she should have been sliding down a stripper pole. In the front row, a guy was sleeping and snoring loudly and it wasn't Sir-Snore-A-Lot or Peter Power Nap. One of our overweight lovers decided to wear his son's elementary school clothes that were five times too small. And, to add insult to injury, he brought what appeared to be a Scooby-Doo lunch pail. All interviewers, including my friend Luke, were shocked to witness such a circus-like atmosphere.

If that wasn't enough to immediately cancel the remaining interviews, one of the first interviewees was drinking a product from one of the bottling company's main competitors. As my friend was describing this scene to me, I was sitting at my desk stunned. I reassured him that we didn't prepare, encourage nor endorse that ridiculously unprofessional circus-like behavior. Needless to say, my friend and his bosses decided not to move forward with our collaborative recruitment hiring partnership. I wholeheartedly apologized to my friend regarding that unfortunate incident and vowed to never ever bring up partnership collaboration with our organization. To this day, Luke and I remain the best of friends. We were once college roommates sharing many fun collegiate moments; both of our teenage sons were born in the same year and only eight days apart. So, do you think for a moment that the unfortunate performance by our shamefully embarrassing PTs would permanently damage our friendship? Nope! Not gonna happen.

The major lesson I learned from that unfortunate incident was that one can pretty much hand someone on a frickin' silver platter– an employment opportunity that could change their lives; however, if they don't act like they have some damn common professional sense and really want it, then all the incredible life-changing employment opportunities are truly in vain!!!

Later on that year, in 1998, another employer partnership opportunity came about from a company that was one of the nation's leaders in inbound/outbound telecommunications. A meeting was set up between the office supervisor, hiring manager, and me regarding a partnership between them and our organization that would potentially bring hundreds of job opportunities for our PTs in their ever growing/expanding company. After the major bottling company debacle, I reserved my excitement until we got past the initial hires. The inbound caller positions were perfect for anyone who enjoyed talking to people, data entry, dispatching, typing, and additional customer service oriented duties. The pre-requisites for the position were very reasonable—a high school diploma/GED preferred (however, transcripts reflecting a significant completion of high school credits were acceptable), no criminal background check, no drug test, type at least 25 wpm, pass a basic third grade level mathematics exam, and overall, be friendly, courteous, professional…

Every week for the next six months, Allen, the hiring manager, and his staff would come to one of our L.A. sites and provide a brief orientation, conduct first round interviews, invite a small percentage of the exceptional candidates to the final interview round held at the corporate office in Culver City, CA. By the end of the first month, over 30 of our PTs were HIRED! I couldn't believe the amazing success we were having. Month after month after month the jobs kept coming in, 30-35 on average. We were literally rolling in the jobs! It was incredible to see this unfolding before our very eyes. It felt like I was in Vegas at one of the crap tables rolling nothing but sevens and elevens, with a cigar in my mouth, a beautiful woman hanging on my arm, a large crowd around cheering us on, while receiving high-roller comp treatment, and the limo driver waiting outside for me and my female guest to take us out for a fun night out on the town…

It was a perfect marriage between us and the company. They had hundreds of expansion jobs to fill, and we were their only hiring source! They didn't advertise via the *L.A. Times*, EDD, leading staffing agencies, or any other applicant pool sources. My colleagues were also ecstatic because job placements were at an all-time high, morale was through the roof, and the overall office environment was awesome!

Well, as they say, all good things eventually come to an end, and boy did it ever come to a crashing end! A little after seven months of having tremendous job placement success with this company, I received a call from Allen saying, "Hello Jahi how are you?"

"Fine," I replied, "and you?"

He said well, "You may wanna sit down for this one. I have some bad news to tell you." As he began sharing how two of our recently hired PTs got into a physical altercation in the company parking lot, and one of them pulled out a knife and stabbed the other one, my heart dropped!

I responded by repeating at least 12 times, "Oh my God! You got to be kidding?" No, he wasn't kidding! He said the paramedics came and rushed the stabbed victim to the emergency room and the perpetrator was immediately arrested. Nevertheless, the company called an emergency staff meeting and decided to sever its relationship with us. Unbeknownst to me, there were a large number of our employed PTs who had punctuality, attendance, performance and interpersonal relationships problems; there were various other challenges, and they had been given several warnings to improve overall work ethics or face likely termination. I literally had neither inclination nor clue that many of our hired PT's displayed those unprofessional work ethics, during that seven month period. Allen opted not to inform me about those inappropriate staff behavioral challenges because they were in-house company issues and he didn't want to burden me with work related issues that the company could handle internally. However, the stabbing incident was the straw that broke the camel's back. I responded by apologizing several times and I also reiterated how extremely disappointed I was regarding our ungrateful, unappreciative, un-thankful, selfish, ignorant-ass PTs…

I was lividly pissed! I said, "How dare these idiots! They ruined a good thing! Those morons just blew it for future PTs who could have had employment opportunities." On behalf of the company, Allen apologized about severing our agreement and wished me the best of luck. I ended the conversation by thanking him and the entire company for giving our organization and the PTs these employment opportunities.

The very next year, in late 1999, our organization recognized him and his company in a very nice award ceremony honoring companies who hired a significant percentage of our PTs; of which, his company hired over 230 during the 1998-1999 fiscal year. It was our organization's way of expressing our appreciation for companies giving our PTs employment opportunities. I again expressed my deepest apologies for the unfortunate way our partnership ended; however, I reminded them that by employing this population, it's another step in the right direction, in hopes that one day all of our welfare-to-work PTs will transition off public assistance, and enter/re-enter the workforce and become invaluable contributors to themselves, their families, communities, nation, and world…

CHAPTER 5: *The Big Four*

As 1999 came to a close, I was optimistic that the new millennium would bring much greater employment success for all of our PTs. However, an unfortunate trend in the wrong direction really began to surface. The year was 2000! The Lakers had won the first of what would be a NBA championship "three-peat-feat," and the Rams took their "Greatest Show On Turf" to a Super Bowl win, the Yankees would complete their own "three- peat-feat version," our country witnessed the United States Supreme Court decide the fate of the most unusual presidential election ever. Yet many of us on the front line at our various sites began noticing the overall conditions/barriers of our PTs worsening as the subsequent years progressed. And over the next five years, barriers to employment such as mental health, substance abuse, transitional living, and felony convictions exploded to unprecedented heights for a significant percentage of our PTs.

Its summer of 2005 and one of our classes totally exemplified this explosion of change during this period. Out of 25 enters, more than half the class acknowledged felony convictions as barriers to employment on the first day. Each day garnered a different incident. The first Tuesday, of the first week, witnessed two rival gang members squaring off to fight one another in one of our classrooms with the accompaniment of our tables/chairs. One of our female security guards was physically assaulted during the fight break-up. Wednesday of that same week witnessed our security guards confiscate knives, razor blades, switch blades, box cutters, and additional weaponry of choice prior to PTs entering classrooms. The trend that I began to see was that there was a growing influx of PTs who were dealing with some severe barriers to employment such as felony convictions, substance abuse, mental health, homelessness. As the PTs were dealing with their barriers, employers were beginning to rapidly change their employment description requirements. Many companies began to require a minimum high school diploma/GED, no felony convictions, mental health application test questionnaires, and passage of a drug test. These are what I call the "Big Four" reasons why many of our PTs don't obtain employment.

I remember a time back in the late 1980s where a job seeker could walk into a McDonald's restaurant in shorts, flip-flops, a "wife-beater" tank top, and uncombed hair, fill out an application, have an on-the-spot interview, and get the job offer. Those days are long gone now! Applicants often go through a very rigorous online application process before they ever even get an interview opportunity. Now look at this formula for a significant percentage of our PTs: No high school diploma/G.E.D + Felony Record + Mental Health + Substance Abuse= ? Yep! You guessed it, a very challenging population to serve! Nonetheless, they are able-bodied and capable of earning a legal/legitimate living. Let's start with the ones who have no high school diploma/GED. More often than not, they have other barriers coupled with this educational challenge such as substance abuse and/or felony convictions.

One of the things my colleagues and I always remind PTs is that literally every community has a local adult school, community college, trade school, vocational school, or church that offer GED classes. It's up to them to at least enroll in one of the schools and get the ball rolling. Therefore, when a company advertises a job lead and the minimum education requirements states: must have high school diploma/ GED–hello!–many of them are automatically disqualified from interview consideration and a subsequent job offer. This leads us into the JSPC classes where there BIG Four Challenges are totally exposed. Remember, that 100% of ALL of our PTs who enter our JSPC component are deemed employable! Nonetheless, on the first day of JSPC, each instructor gets a feel for the types of barriers to employment each PT faces from class participation or completion of paperwork. Oftentimes, a PT simply confesses their illiterate challenges via private sidebar conversations. Under CALWORKS, all PTs must go through the JSPC component, unless a legitimate medical condition temporarily/ permanently exempts them from working. An illiterate PT is still considered an employable PT under the current CALWORKS by-laws. A typical day number one of JSPC dress code looks something like this: exaggerated oversized baggy garment wear displayed, flip-flops/sandals, sweat-suits, exercise outfits, stripper gear, shorts, stereotypical gang-affiliated attire, excessively large t-shirts, and additional inappro-priate/unprofessional job-readiness clothing wardrobe. I mean, seri-ously! Many of our PTs come dressed as if they were going to the beach, park, or back-yard barbeque, but not professional job searching! As we discuss the dress code each PT must adhere to beginning week two, MANY of them object to the dress code due to one unanimous reason: they allegedly don't have the dress code attire we require. Therefore, DPSS issues them an additional $50-$70 for what falls under a clothing voucher and grooming/hygiene assistance. Let's take a closer look at what PTs receive on their EBT benefits.

On the GAIN side (Custodial Parent PTs), they receive on average between $500-$600 dollars monthly of state/federal grant money. The majority of these custodial PTs also qualify for an incredibly reduced child care stipend where they'll save up to 50% or more of savings on child care rate charges. Those of us who are parents know very well how expensive childcare is! A segment of our PTs were/are or will be receiving section 8 housing. To give you a quick example of how this works, let's say a PT is renting a two-bedroom, two-bath section 8 apartment that rents for $1200 a month. More than likely, the PT will pay between $80-$120 dollars a month in rent; however, guess who pays the remaining $1080-$1120 each and every month? You guessed it! We the Taxpayers do! Not to mention the free weekly Metro Tran-sit Authority (MTA) bus pass that at least 85-90% of our PTs receive weekly. Last time I checked, that's another $17-$20 a week. Wonder-ing what the other 10-15% of PTs do about transportation cost? No need to worry–they receive a comparable amount in gas expenses. That's right–they get gas money. But wait! There's more! Our PTs also qualify for Homeless Court Forgiveness Debt Relief. Let's say a PT has outstanding unpaid misdemeanor citations such as parking, jay-walking, MTA ride violations up to thousands of dollars that will be totally dismissed or paid for compliments of–guess who?–Taxpayer Dollars! Even if the initial misdemeanor citations turned into warrants! We're talking about hundreds and even thousands of dollars paid for by hard-working taxpayers! Our PTs also get free internet access for job search purposes, endless copies of job search related documents, phone usage, and additional complimentary services.

Now, one would think that all of our PTs would express gratitude, thankfulness, and overall appreciation for all these services and benefits provided to them right? Wrong! Generally, right after welcoming/ice-breaker activities, many of our PTs gripe or complain about not getting enough help from the county…can you believe the nerve? The audacity that any of them complain about not getting enough county assistance when we have Americans pushing shopping cart baskets down city streets by day and sleeping on park benches by night. What nerve of them complaining when most states in our country don't offer as much welfare supportive services and benefits that's given to them here in California. How dare they gripe when we still see heartfelt images of children in third world impoverished nations, with imploded bellies, literally starving around our earth that is rich in natural minerals/resources etc. And, way too many of these grown adults still feel entitled to receive above and beyond what's already allocated to them? Absolutely incredible! My mind still can't process this thinking…

As we get through the typical first day of JSPC, day two is generally designated for developing a PT profile which consists of identifying barriers to employment, goal-setting, items needed for job search support, an overall game plan to transition them into/back into the workforce. During the application workshop, we generally further identify the challenges listed in their profile forms, which consist of the usual felony convictions, homelessness, substance abuse, and mental health barriers. We have both individual and group class participatory activities. For the PTs dealing with felony records, they often ask how we can help them get jobs. This typically isn't a cut and dried answer because there are several factors that play a role in their employment success. First of all, we inform them about the weekly felony expungement workshops that provide legal assistance in expunging certain felonies. However, certain felonies are non-expunge-able, such as murder/manslaughter, sexual assaults, child molestation, and certain drug-trafficking cases. Each class differs regarding the amount of PTs with felony records. However, it's not unusual to have a class where up to 50% or more have felony convictions within the last 10 years. And, most companies conduct a 7-10 year criminal background check where felony convictions often disqualify them from even getting interviews-much less a job offer. Therefore, many of these PTs often become frustrated with the overall job market.

I also remind PTs that it's often about re-packaging their brand image to employers. What could I possibly mean by this? It's like a car that needs an entire rebuilt/new engine and body frame detailing replacement. It hasn't quite made it to the scrap/junkyards deemed unsalvageable, yet it desperately needs a total engine/body-frame overhaul. Whether they're seeking physical blue-collar work or white-collar office environment work, quite often they don't look-the-part, talk the part, nor are they prepared for same day interviews, which means they're going to have to invest countless hours in repackaging/re-branding their professional job-seeker image. They're job search-ing wearing hats, shorts, t-shirts and baggy casual wear, or other inap-propriate attire. Some are wannabe plumbers with no certifications/licenses, pictures of work, or networking contacts of plumbers in the industry. Others want construction work, but can't tell the difference between a straight and Phillips screw-driver. And, then there are those who want to do office work but have no professional office etiquette.

I explain to them that developing their brand starts with the sim-ple basic fundamentals of their respective profession, then you build a marketable product called "Professional Marketable Self Image" (PMSI) that can compete for those jobs. It takes a lot of initial sacri-ficing, patience, consistency. Building/rebuilding of their brand, and a little creative ingenuity to get to that point. One of many examples of this that I share when I facilitate JSPC workshop classes is the time when I assisted my longtime college friend and his family move out of San Diego, California. As the four of us began what turned out to be an entire weekend long marathon move, we all realized that we needed to hire some local movers who could provide additional mov-ing muscle strength to help expedite the process. We went down to the neighborhood Home Depot, and three guys immediately approached our U-Haul truck. We informed them about the details of the move, negotiated the pay, and hired them for a few hours. It turned out that all three of them made a living as movers five to six days a week. Each one had different barriers to employment such as felony convictions, immigration, child support arrears. Nevertheless, no one allowed their personal challenges to stop them from earning a legal legitimate living. They each earned on average over $100 a day, five to six days a week during the weekdays and a minimum of $120 a day each during the weekends. So I often encourage our felony PTs to look into various legal ways to earn a living via self-employment until time passes when the 7-10 year background check isn't a major factor for employment.

For those PTs who claim homelessness, the county offers emergency shelter vouchers and low-income housing assistance (section 8 housing). What is the case, more often than not, is that a PT is going through a circumstantial living situation, meaning that there's a roof over their heads, food in the cabinets/fridge, and a place to bathe/sleep; however, it's not the healthiest or most ideal living environment. Maybe there's domestic violence, substance abuse, unsafe living conditions, etc. going on that causes them to consider themselves homeless. My true definition of a homeless person is the one we see pushing a shopping cart basket down the street, with their entire belongings in tote, by day, sleeping on park benches and/or park grasses or bus stop benches by night. We often recommend consultation with their eligibility worker for a potential housing referral appt. Some take advantage of these services and others opt not to.

There's been an enormous influx of mental health cases that have entered our JSPC sites between 2005-present. From diagnoses such as depression, anger-management, or bipolar disorder, our hands are truly tied regarding successfully transitioning them into employment. Our mental health staff does a fantastic job in providing quality services, and most of the severe cases are immediately referred to psychiatric evaluation; unfortunately, it's often either not discovered or the PT doesn't admit to their unstable conditions during the initial eligibility process prior to Orientation classes. Some PTs are master disguisers of their mental health conditions. Nevertheless, it always surfaces during our JSPC workshops because we spend so many hours per day together, and their true colors are eventually exposed. Here are a few of the many mental health break-downs we've experienced:

- One young lady was only receiving EBT benefits so she could save up enough money to sue Julia Roberts for allegedly stealing her screenplay idea, which turned into a hit movie.
- Another young man claimed to be a part of our U.S. government's secret Pentagon mission operation, preparing for battle with our enemies in the universe; therefore, he couldn't get a job here on earth.
- One guy was so pissed off at us that he rammed his car full speed ahead into the side of our building, with a cubicle desk right in harm's way. Fortunately, no one was injured.

We've had countless other incidents where PTs angrily cursed us out, threatened to harm us, kill us, and blow up the county building. Substance abuse is a very common barrier our PTs face. We remind them that there are substance abuse treatment services, with highly qualified/certified substance abuse counselors, where they can receive quality services, compliments of taxpayers. However, most PTs fail to take advantage of these free services offered to them, for various individual reasons. These services are very important because the majority of companies administer drug tests. The top two chemical substances they are looking for are the cocaine chemical and tetrahydrocannabinol (thc), aka pot, weed, Buddha, mary- jane, herb, dope, schwag, refer, indoor, ooh wee, sticky icky, etc. You know which one is the crowd favorite, right? If you guessed Snoop Dogg's favorite meal of the day, you guessed right! Ding! Ding! Ding! Marijuana. Some of our PTs share their underground tricks to clean out thc from their systems, while others feel it's unfair that businesses single out weed as their top two disqualifiers for obtaining employment. Nonetheless, every class experiences PTs who either fail the drug test or they don't even bother following through with job search procedures due to the inevitable end results. Other substances that either adversely or have a bearing on the success of their job searches are alcohol and certain medications that affect overall coherency.

CHAPTER 6: *Applications*

This leads us to the application workshops. Allow me to illustrate how we present, instruct, and provide invaluable application workshops on how to effectively/professionally fill out job applications.

The first thing we do is have each PT fill out a practice application so that we can evaluate whether or not they know how to correctly complete a typical job application. Next, we facilitate a very thorough workshop providing them with all the essential trade secrets of completing professional job applications. Finally, by the end of the first week, we have them submit a final master application version, which is supposed to be error free and darn near perfect, right? Wrong! It amazes me how we can give them all the most invaluable techniques, terminology, verbiage/language, vernacular, reference guides, inside trade secrets, and examples of how to effectively fill out an application, yet far too many still find a way to incorrectly complete applications!

Let's start with the personal information section. We first address the realization that the majority of job applications are completed online or via a company kiosk system; therefore, most PTs won't have to worry about legibility/penmanship. Our staff reviews both practice applications/final draft version for proofreading corrections/suggestions on improving overall quality of the application. Regarding personal information, we instruct them to thoroughly, specifically, accurately and completely fill out each section. Now, one would think that a person should know the correct spelling of the street one resides on right? Wrong! PTs commonly misspell street names or incorrectly use abbreviations for address. One of our PTs not only used incorrect abbreviations for his home address, but he also misspelled the very street he lived on. Instead of using the proper number abbreviation (#), he spelled out the word number and spelled "Figueroa" as such: "Figeuroa." So it read: blank, blank, number, Figeuroa street. When I brought this to his attention, he responded, "Ah that ain't no big deal, you're being too picky. The work people don't care about that stuff."

After a few times of patiently explaining to him the importance of correcting these mistakes, FP had to come to the rescue…

FP responded, "Dude! You're joking, right? You can't be serious now? First of all, these work people are called 'employers.' They pretty much determine if you're going to even get an interview based upon how impressed or depressed they are after reading this hot mess. Secondly, I have never seen anyone ever spell out the word number as part of their permanent/mailing address. Thirdly, you misspelled the Frickin Street you live on! Dude, you see the Big Ass street sign with the correct spelling of 'Figueroa' on it every day when you leave and return to your crib [house]. You still don't know how to spell the name of the street you live on? Dude, I would strongly suggest you take my professional advice and make the appropriate corrections."

PTs are also required to correct any invalid California ID's/suspended driver's license at the local DMV as part of their active job search. Nevertheless, countless of them have either no current/valid California ID/ driver's license as a result of a suspension and or revocation via the DMV. We advise them to specifically state the exact job title/position they're applying for so employers know they've taken the professional time to research the available positions that company is hiring for. So let's say a retail department store has an entry level Sales Associate position available. I've seen people write "open," "anything," "entry level," "customer service," "sales person," or other inappropriate answers. One guy wrote, "whatever ya'll got." Wait! It gets better: This young man spelled it, "whuteva yaw gat." Yes, he did! Needless to say, this particular guy had other application writing issues. So the correctable advice given would state, "Sales Associate." For the start date section, they're instructed to insert/write the exact month, day, and year, they submit the application for the following reasons. First and foremost, a job application is a legal document. When an applicant electronically and or hard-copy signs/dates that application, the applicant verifies that all information provided is herein true and verifiable for future hiring, verification, and dismissal purposes. Also, it serves as a tracking mechanism for opening/closing dates of positions, complies with state/federal employment regulations, meets contractual obligations for those businesses receiving state/federal funding, etc. So instead of stating the exact month, day, year for start date, I've seen everything from "ASAP" "now," "right now," "today" (like when the hell is today?), "immediately," "whenever yah need me," "only Monday-Friday" (like you can really dictate shifts), "at this moment," etc.

For the work history section, we teach our PTs to gather all pertinent past employment information. We inform them about community resources where they can obtain records of their employment history such as the Employment Development Department (EDD) or Social Security office. They can simply contact their former places of employment via phone, email or internet. Somehow, some way, it's up to them to retrieve their past work history information. Shouldn't be that difficult for them, right? Wrong! It never ceases to amaze me, all of the excuses many of them come up with regarding incomplete/inaccurate information they provide. We remind them that if they don't take the professional time to research/retrieve their own application information, why in the world should/would an employer want to waste his/her, time interviewing them? Employers can pick and choose the best applications from hundreds/thousands they receive for interview/hiring purposes. Hello! It's an employers market! Money's time and time is money. In the work history section, we advise them to include all paid, self-employment, and volunteerism. Dates of employment seem to be a general problem. It amazes me how many of our PTs have partial/incorrect dates. We instruct them to contact their local EDD, Social Security office, or call their former companies for accurate employment dates.

One PT had me so frustrated with pulling this information out of him that I had to have FP step-in and handle it. This particular PT couldn't remember the dates of his past employment for nothing! And, after several minutes of patiently and professionally attempting to have him provide info, FP stepped in and said, "Look dude! Was Jimmy Carter President? Were you sporting a Jeri-Curl? Help me out and give me some kind of time frame of reference." Believe it or not, he still couldn't give me a general time frame of reference. FP instructed him to contact EDD/Social Security office, a.s.a.p. Instead of putting building number, street name, city, and state for the address of one of his previous jobs, one of our PTs put, "It's right across the street from the fish fry spot next to Nix check-cashing."

FP: "Come on, man Are you giving directions to cousin Pookie and Nem? Or are you filling out a job application?"

Reasons for leaving employment responses are often quite telling. One young lady cited a back injury from sliding down a stripper pole, another guy got fired after getting caught on hidden video surveillance camera stuffing product items in his jacket. And, one young lady said she had relocated. When I asked her where she relocated from, she replied, "From Lynwood to Compton, CA."

I told her girlfriend, "You can't tell employers that you relocated from Lynwood, CA to Compton, CA because they're right next door to each other, hello!"

Too often, our PTs leave out way too much detailed information that a company uses to determine how polished a potential interviewee candidate presents him/herself. Names of companies should be spelled correctly with accurate addresses, phone numbers, and dates of employment. The common excuses we've heard about why this information is inaccurate and/or incomplete are:

- It was so long ago that I forgot.
- I didn't know I had to give them the complete address–cross streets won't do? (FP: Nor will landmarks do.)
- They just axing for too much. (FP: yeah, that's why they're employers–because they can! By the way, the word is "asking," not "axing"!)
- My phone number is disconnected. (We always recommend that they temporarily use a family member, friend, significant other, neighbor, etc.)

We've also had countless terminations due to alcohol/illegal substance consumptions. Also, I've seen some very interesting responses on the education sections. PTs have misspelled the names of the very high schools they've attended such as "Moaninside," for Morningside High School in Inglewood, California. For dates attended, one guy wrote, "Back in the 80s" instead of putting month/year for graduation date, he put, "Not yet." Yes, he did. They unanimously leave out so much detailed information such as full complete names of colleges, trade schools, training programs, credits, certifications and or degrees received, dates attended, completed/graduated, etc. Regarding references, we strongly advise that they use references that they've known for at least one year; the references will provide a professional endorsement in the areas of employment, education, and volunteerism. What do we quite often get? One PT used a reference where the phone was disconnected, email address invalid; mailing address incomplete. I asked him, "How in the hell are employers gonna get in touch with this reference?"

The answer I got was, "They just gone have to wait until he gets out of jail!"

Now, you know FP had to handle this right? FP: "Employers ain't got time to charge a collect call through an operator for a California Corrections Institute! And, they damn sure don't wanna talk to Ray-Ray who's serving time for robbery! Hello!"

PTs are also reminded to keep in touch with their references on a fairly regular basis until they obtain employment. However, it's not unusual to have a reference totally forget who the hell they are! The majority of applications are being completed online or via the company's in-house kiosk system; more and more companies are including psychological evaluation type questionnaires to further gain an assessment of the applicant's overall professional proto-type profile.

Class sessions are typically three to four hours in length, with a 15-minute break included. They are not allowed to be absent during the first week of instruction, unless the following occurs to themselves: death, life-support in ICU, judicial/court notices, and company letterhead/email interview invitations. We also give them a 30-minute grace period to get to class before they're considered late/tardy. It's important for them to understand the relevance of punctuality and attendance, because employers pay very close attention to these two areas during a new hires probationary period. So we want our PTs to start practicing good habits in class so that they can transfer those good habits into their new respective places of employment. Here are just a few tardiness/absenteeism excuses we've heard over the years during the first week of JSPC (of course, FP chimes in via the parenthesis following each excuse):

1. The bus came late/broke-down.
2. I was in the "bafroom." (Not bathroom or restroom, but baf-room.)
3. I was running all the way from my house.
4. I didn't know class started at this time.
5. I over-slept.
6. I had to take my meds.
7. I got chased by rival gang members.
8. The security line was too long.
9. I got pulled over/harassed by the cops.
10. "I ain't gone even lie dawg, I'm just late."

The excuses for absences include:

1. My significant other locked me out of the house. (We offer domestic violence services to PTs who use this excuse; how-ever, they usually decline services).
2. I got stuck in Tijuana Mexico.
3. I had food poisoning (but won't get doctor's excuse).
4. I got arrested/violated probation or parole.
5. I over-slept. (For 3-4 hours?)
6. I had to take a family member to their doctor's appointment.
7. I had diarrhea. (Can't provide medical note.)
8. I was cramping bad (PMS).
9. I lost my inhaler.
10. I was held in S&M bondage by my significant other. (Once again, domestic violence services are offered.)
11. I had an interview. (But can't provide verifiable proof.)
12. I had to attend my family reunion. (For the 3rd time in the same year.)
13. I was observing my country's religious observance, (However, the religion they mentioned wasn't observing that day.)
14. I forgot to take my temporary memory loss prescription.
15. There was a big drug bust in my complex; it was all over the news.
16. I got an STD after going to this happy hour spot. (Aren't Happy Hour spots for working folk?)

17. I couldn't find my contacts/glasses.
18. I went to a job fair, (However, can't provide any proof of attendance.)
19. I just needed a day off (So PTs accrue sick/vacation time?), but I'm ready to go back to class.
20. The class is boring, I already know this stuff. (Yet you keep repeating this boring class.)
21. I had some "impotant thangs" to do. (Maybe "impotant thangs" are a little more serious than "important things"!)
22. I had to take my kid to the amusement park for their birthday. (On taxpayers' dollars? That couldn't have waited until the weekend?)
23. I ain't gone lie to ya'll, I just didn't feel like coming. (But I bet you feel just fine swiping that EBT card, huh?)
24. Ya'll cut my benefits, as soon as ya'll put my benefits back on, I'll be back in class. (This ignorant ass excuse doesn't even deserve a response.)

We instruct our PTs to maintain a final version of an error-free master application and save it in their portfolios. Here's a quick note regarding portfolios! We strongly recommend that they either keep one of our portfolios or invest in their own so they can keep copies of very important documents such as pre-printed, error-free master applications; diplomas; degrees; certifications; DMV records; court documents; recommendation letters; awards/achievements; references; head-shot photos (entertainment industry); pictures of finished general contractor projects (construction); business cards; writing utensils, etc. Therefore, whether a PT is filling out an application online for Toyota Motor Corp of America, via the kiosk at Macy's, or in person at Wing Stop, all they'd have to do is transfer or copy down the error-free pre-written master application information onto the respective company's application format. Now, God only knows what's really happening when they leave our workshops to go fill out the company's application? To be a fly on-the-wall, and see what's really going on out there in the field…

One employer asked us during a career fair if we were properly instructing these PTs on how to fill out a job application. I responded by inviting him to sit in on any of our application workshops and see for himself. Not to brag, but our application, resume, and interview workshops are on a world class level! I'd venture to say that most CEOs would be very impressed!

CHAPTER 7: *Resumes*

Resume workshops are usually a lot of fun for our PTs because we break them up into groups and literally dissect a few different group-assigned resume format versions, from the heading down to the references section. After dissecting their group-assigned resumes, they record all of the errors, mistakes, corrections, and any identified enhancement findings onto a flip-chart paper to be presented in front of the entire class at the end of the workshop. In essence, they get a chance to do a little role reversal and put themselves in the shoes of a pre-screening personnel/human resource staff. They also get to brainstorm all findings with fellow class-mates; those that have stage-fright get an opportunity to take a small step in overcoming their public speaking fears. Finally, each group presents their findings as the facilitator is systematically going over the correctable suggestions for each section of each group-assigned resume. So by the time the PTs complete this resume workshop, they receive strategic instructions on how to effectively advertise themselves on paper along with invaluable marketable tips, with the end result of effectively developing their own resume masterpieces. After all this, what do we typically get? Some crazy-ass stuff we never taught them to do. Let's take a closer look at some resume post-workshop presentation examples.

In the heading section, we instruct them to make sure that their names stand out by using larger font sizes and bolding the letters. Also, their phone numbers and email addresses should be eye-catching. The examples I always give in my workshops are: Your name should have that Las Vegas effect–LARGE. BOLD. BIG! GO BIG OR GO HOME! The original architects of these phenomenal casinos realized that by creating enormous buildings with big lights highlighting the names of the hotels/casinos so guest/visitors exiting the freeways would get excited about jumping out of those limos, buses, trucks, sport utility vehicles, cars, and wanna race into the casinos to gamble, shop, watch shows, concerts, special events, or enjoy family entertainment. Our names should have that same exciting effect! Next, we strongly advise our

PTs to have professional outgoing music messages, preferably with no lyrics! I've heard way too many crazy outgoing messages over the years. One guy used a hip-hop song track laced with profanity, vulgarity, and disrespect to women. After employers finish listening to all that profanity, inappropriate ethnic slurs, and derogatory language disrespecting women, they'll then hear this fool say, "Ya'll know who dis is, leave one." The average employer would've hung up after the first few seconds of all that nonsense. Email addresses should also be professional. One of our young ladies' email address was Bigblacksexyboodie@blah, blah, blah.com! I told her, "Young-Lady, you can't use that email address unless you're applying for a position in a gentlemen's club/strip club."

She responded, "Oh please Jahi. I've gotten jobs before with this email."

I replied, "Unless the job duties have something to do with giving lap dances and sliding down a stripper pole, don't use that email address. We want to make sure you're appropriately marketable to a wide variety of employers." Her response was neither here nor there; nevertheless, it reflects how way too many of our PTs don't incorporate our teachings into their resume enhancement techniques. Too often, our PTs use what I call a "generic" objective–something like: "Seeking a position with a company where I can utilize my skills, training, knowledge, abilities, and expertise, and be a part of a growing company." We instruct them to identify specific position/s applied for, state name of company, and let them know you'll be a good long-term investment. Here's how I'd rephrase this objective. Let's say I was applying for an entry-level sales related position at Macy's. My objective would state: "To obtain a Sales Associate position within Macy's corporation-with the opportunity for career advancement." So, I'm identifying the specific job title/position for which I'm applying, stating the name of the company, and letting them know that I'll be a good long-term investment. The thing that never ceases to amaze me is that our PTs can't remember the information of the companies they worked for, nor can they articulate the work experience they allegedly have/had. Once again, too many of our PTs have a very difficult time with this section. Give you a couple of examples. One young lady allegedly had 10 years of experience taking care of our senior citizen/elderly population in a residential setting. Now I've never actually worked in that profession; however, I've met many people who have done this type of work over the years, so I've learned some of the terminology/lingo of that industry. When she attempted to describe her job title and duties, it was a hot mess with no bacon grease! Here's how she described her particular experience: "I helped old people with thangs, clean around da house, I get em stuff and give em pills." When I read this I was flabbergasted!

I asked her, "Do you really have 10 years of experience in this field?" She answered, "Yeah! Why, you don't believe me?"

I said to be quite honest, "NO! First of all, most people who've been in this industry for the amount of years you claim know how to describe their experience using the buzz words/terminology of your profession."

Here's how I suggested she rephrase her duties: provided quality senior, and/or elderly adult care services which included: administered medications, prepared meals, performed cleaning duties such as swept/mopped floors, dusted shelves/furniture items, vacuumed rooms, sanitized bathrooms, scheduled and transported patients to/from medical appointments, coordinated indoor/outdoor entertainment activities, and provided family of patient with daily activity progress reports." It's quite often not what they say, but how they say it on paper that could make a difference between getting interviews and not getting interviews.

It reminded me about one of my many collegiate jobs. In college, I had 23 different roommates, lived in nine different residences, and mowed through 12 different jobs. I was a collegiate hustler, to say the least. Nothing was going to stop me from getting that degree! One of my favorite college jobs was when I was a Maintenance Engineer for my university's dormitory housing complex. It was such a blast! My job title sounded very prominent, huh? Actually, I did janitorial work and light housing maintenance work. My job duties consisted of: emptying garbage, power-spraying grounds/walkways; sweeping trash/debris from stairs, balconies, and tri-level parking structure; plunging toilets; unclogging sinks; installing light fixtures; reporting electrical, mechanical, and product-related malfunctions for service repair orders; basically, maintaining overall cleanliness of entire building grounds. Some of the perks/fringe benefits of that job came when we would enter student dorm suites to perform work orders. Upon completing a work order, I regularly received offers/invitations from some of the female resident students, which included having meals prepared while viewing Oprah shows; music listening sessions; playing the role of Dr. Phil while I listened to their boyfriend problems; playing card/board games; and sexual advances/encounters. One day this young hot freshman that I had my eye on for an entire semester came out of the bathroom shower with a really sexy bath robe on, and her silky black hair was dripping wet. After she gave me the longest hug greeting, wonder what might have happened next? You guessed it! Upon the pleasurably successful completion of fixing her leaky pipes, she took a well deserved nap, then I kissed her on the forehead and raced downstairs to our maintenance office, only to find out that the maintenance office had closed, everyone had left for the evening, and I had no way of getting inside the alarm-censored building.

The next day my supervisor asked me why I failed to clock out the day before. I came up with an emergency plumbing excuse. I told him that I lost track of time as I was unclogging/repairing some leaky pipes. Not too far from the truth, right? So for the remainder of that semester, remarkably, I had to go to this young lady's suite at least two or three times a week and perform various work orders such as readjusting bed frames, installing bedroom light-fixtures, tightening shower/tub heads, resetting the garbage disposal system, providing complimentary dish washing instructions, and additional emergency orders that needed my immediate service attention. Well, enough about my extra-curricular collegiate escapades for now, back to our Ms. Help Old People with Thangs!

One would think that after giving her a more professional way to rephrase her duties, that she would graciously receive my suggestions with open arms, right? Wrong! She responded by saying, "Thanks, Jahi, but I feel better using my own words."

I replied, "Ok! Best wishes in your quest to obtain a rewarding Senior/Elder Adult Care-Provider position."

Another one of our PTs described his warehouse duties like two pre-school children fighting over crayons and Lego pieces—it was not nice! First of all, dude incorrectly spelled the company name, forgot dates of employment, failed to use specific job title, unprofessionally listed job duties, and provided inaccurate dates of employment. Once again, between EDD, Social Security office, General Operator Info, and the Internet, there is no excuse not to provide companies with accurate, specific, verifiable information! I did warehouse work for Honda Motor Corporation during my collegiate era; I remember the warehouse terminology was very specific to industry standards. But he described his duties as "load car stuff and move things around." The dates only stated 2004-2005, and he listed an inappropriate reason for leaving the company. Now this was Toyota Motor Corporation of America! First of all, he spelled the company name "Toy-ota." I asked him, "How on God's beautiful green earth did you get that particular spelling? Did you not see the big ass "TOYOTA" sign plastered on that big ole building in gigantic letters every time you went to work? And you still found a way to misspell their name? Did you not look up at the name of the company as you entered the building? TOYOTA is one of the leading automotive manufacturing companies in the United States of America, and one of the global leaders in this international market. I can assure you that they would be professionally insulted if they saw this mess." I strongly suggested that he retrieve accurate dates of employment by calling Toyota's HR department and requesting his dates of employment history in writing/via phone, or take a trip down to the local EDD/Social Security office and retrieve print-outs of work history.

To add insult to injury, want to guess how he spelled one of McDonald's main restaurant competitors? "Jack and The Bx." I responded by saying, "Hold up! Isn't the correct spelling of Jack's internationally known restaurant Jack In The Box?" He responded, "I don't know man, I guess!" I replied, "Didn't you allegedly work there for six months according to the dates listed on your application? What compelled you to add the word, 'and,' inside the company name, where nowhere on this planet earth is Jack's restaurant spelled the way you spell it?" He had no logical response worth repeating; therefore, I strongly suggested that he Google up the accurate spelling of both Toyota and Jack In The Box corporate restaurant names prior to inserting that information into future job applications. Now when it came to describing his duties, I attempted to use one of my favorite sports analogy examples. I said, "When a sports announcer provides play-by-play commentary for a game, they use professional sports terminology that's relative to the respective sport in reference." My all-time favorite sports commentator who was absolutely brilliant at color commentating was Francis Chick Hearn. Chick Hearn gave the best play-by-play professional sports announcement I've ever heard. When Chickie Baby did play-by-play announcing for the Los Angeles Lakers for almost 40 years, he colorfully illustrated the game so that radio listeners could visualize what the television viewers were watching using a combination of his own Chickism language intertwined with the NBA's basketball terminology. A common Chickie baby call would have gone something like this: "Rambis inbounds the ball to Magic being harassed by Pippen, Magic comes across the 10-second line (which is now an 8-second back-court violation line), passes over to Scott on the right-side 22ft out, now guarded by Pippen. Scott takes two dribbles, swings it back over to Magic, Magic top of the circle, yo-yoing up and down, as he backs his man down, one dribble, two dribbles, as he looks up at the clock, no look over-the-shoulder baseline pass to Worthy, Worthy left-side baseline touch pass to Kareem, three feet under the basket turnaround, and SLAM DUNK!" Many of Chick Hearn's terms have been adopted by the NCAA and NBA overseas commentators such as "dribble-drive," "alley-oop," "stutter-step," and the global "SLAM DUNK!" Nevertheless, too many of our PTs fail to digest the terminology/vernacular of their respective profession. So if one can't articulate their expertise within their own profession, where's the believability/credibility and ultimately marketability?

Imagine searching for a new family doctor via your new health care provider coverage plan. You schedule the first routine physical examination check-up with your newly assigned family physician. After the medical staff or nurse does the preliminary weight, vital signs, and chart documentation for physician review, the doctor enters your patient room with a puzzled/perplexed look on his face. The immediate reaction of most of us would be, "What's wrong, Doctor?" Now, if that Doctor begins to stutter, mumble, and not speak the usual medical terminology used by most physicians, wouldn't you be just a little concerned about his credibility as your family physician? I mean, this guy's talking like he received his medical degree from some online crack-pot school that's not accredited by the American Medical Association (AMA), or falsified his way to becoming part of that hospital's medical staff. We would have to question/challenge this physician's legitimacy as a professionally licensed medical doctor, would we not? For the most part, our PTs are just not effectively marketing themselves on paper.

The work history section on resumes is usually another area where PTs quite often leave out too much detailed information. We inform them to use subtitles such as Job, Employment, and/or Work History. They are instructed to include name of company, job title/position held, dates employed, and city/state location. What generally happens? What I've noticed way too often is that many of our PTs don't want to take the professional time to provide thorough and detailed employment information. The education section on resumes is another area where many of our PTs fall way short of effectively advertising their educational accomplishments. We strongly encourage them to include ALL pertinent high school, college, trade school, or vocational school training, whether they completed it or not. If they have yet to complete their certificate, diploma, or degree, we advise them to at least give themselves credit for the duration/dates they attended the aforementioned schools. Some credit is better than no credit at all, right? I want this to be very clear that our PTs submit resume worksheets along with already typed resumes to us. We review all resume submittals by critiquing every word, on every line, within every section, of each PTs resume! However, far too often our PTs don't embrace our professional critique suggestions to make their resumes stand out and become more effective marketing tools for their job search...

References are another problem for our PTs. We remind them NOT to use close family members, people they aren't in regular contact with, or references that will give negative or unprofessional responses. Here are some of the many ill-advised mistakes they've made. One day I called one of our PTs references and her mom answered the phone.

I politely/professionally asked for the name given on the resume, and her mom replied, "That's me!"

I said, "Good afternoon, Ma'am! Did you know that your daughter is using you as a reference?"

Mom answered, "Yes I did!" I responded by telling her that our program doesn't advise your daughter to use such close family members due to the obvious family biased affiliations. Mom began to ask me questions about her own EBT benefits.

I said, "Hold on, Miss. Wait just a minute! You mean to tell me that you're receiving benefits also?"

"Yep, and I'm 'bout to start your class on Monday!!!"

Needless to say, her Mama wasn't exactly a good reference. I perform what I call "robo-calls" to check validity/authenticity of the references they use. So when I made another robo-reference call, this young lady's jealous boyfriend answered the phone with a mean overtone. *Ring!* As he answered the phone, I said, "Good morning, Sir. My name is Jahi, and I'm one of the Career Development Program Specialists for Los Angeles County Office of Education." Before I could say blah, blah, blah is using you as an employment reference, he interrupted me by blurting out, "Who dis?" I repeated myself; this time before I could repeat the Los Angeles County part, he interrupted me again my blurting out, "What chu wont wit her?" Now, 99.9% of employers would have politely ended that conversation with a "Sorry to disturb you– Have a nice day…" As I informed him that blah-blah-blah is using him as an employment reference he responded by saying, "A reference! What for? And, why she using me?" At that point, I decided to end the conversation professionally. Later that day, I received a call from the young lady asking me the details of my conversation with her man. I told her that this is a perfect teachable moment on why it's important to use positive, courteous, professional references that will say good things about you and represent you in a professional manner.

We also remind our PTs that if you use a reference of a particular practicing religious/spiritual faith, make sure you have verifiable information on that person and they know who the HELL you are. One of our older gentlemen used a prominent pastor in the community as a reference and claimed that he was one of the associate ministers serving under the guidance and leadership of this particular pastor. Now, you know this was too good for me to pass up and not check the authenticity of this reference, right? Therefore, I left a message with who I thought was the pastor's voicemail. A few days later, I get a call from the church secretary stating that this particular PT wasn't an associate minister for that church, nor was he even a member of the church. When I confronted our PT with this falsified finding a day or two later, he responded by saying, "I didn't know you guys call and check these references!" FP: "Duh, dude!" I reminded him that more and more employers are checking references as part of the entire application/interview process, so you don't want to practice bad habits by using falsified references.

Once again, as facilitators, we constantly remind our PTs to invest in a binder/portfolio, so that they could keep a pre-printed/pre-written master application, typed resumes, and additional documents and paper-work they may need during their job search, with the least amount of errors as possible, already inserted into the binder as they conduct their daily job search. LACOE offers complimentary portfolios that we distribute to each class. Believe it or not, some PTs reject these free binders, toss them in trash cans, leave them on bus stop benches, or simply forget to bring them to class daily. As I quite often check their portfolios, I see empty, incomplete, insufficient copies in their binders. I also remind them that Suga Free gave us ALL great advice, "If We Stay Ready We Ain't Gotta Get Ready." Now of course, this west coast hip-hop artist was talking about the pimpin'/hustling' lifestyle, but nonetheless, it's really clever advice that's transferable to the job market–for all of us to practice good habits and have copies of EVERY marketable piece of self-advertisement–their PMSI. Some of our PTs have never completed a typed resume. Others just need to make some section updates/enhancements. While some of our PTs have excellent resumes, they typically still learn something new by the end of our workshop. So what is the end result of typed resumes we receive by a large number of our PTs? Upon the completion of these professionally facilitated resume workshops, what kind of typed resumes do they submit to us? Here are a few examples…

One of our young ladies, we'll call her Ms. Seductive, had a very sexually provocative outgoing voicemail message from an R&B track, for what seemed like a minute. Now, as the music was playing, laced with sexually explicit lyrics, you can hear her narrating overtures in the background filled with seductive, sensual, provocative language saying, "What took you so long? I've been waiting for your call…Don't make me wait any longer…Leave a message if you dare"! After hearing Ms. Seductive's message the first time, I was awaiting the prompt stating, for massage press #1, for lap dance press #2. She might as well have added those prompts because I was already envisioning her sliding down a stripper pole while listening to R. Kelly's bump 'n grind remix. Email addresses are a growing problem also. One guy's email says, "Gangstazdontdancetheyboogie@_____.com. What is the perception most employers will have? Exactly—ole boy has a gangbanging' thug life, right? They don't want that potential drama in their company.

The young lady whose email address read, bigblacksexyboodie@blahblahblah.com didn't want to change it because it reflected her personality and style. I must admit, she did have a very nice big "black sexy boodie," but that's beside the point! Therefore, I informed her that unless she was applying for a position in a gentleman's club, her email address would be highly inappropriate to use for the average employer. Most of the PTs responses to constructive resume enhancement advice are that we're having them do too much or that they didn't have time to tailor every resume for every company. My response to this is to save different industry versions on a flash/USB drive, and then make the necessary adjustments/changes for each company applied for via resume submittal. I guess many of our PTs just don't get it, huh? This is the most competitive job market of all time. Yes, the 1929 stock market crash resulted in a 25% national unemployment rate, most industries suffered dearly, and the national suicide rate climbed to unprecedented highs, and I am in no way diminishing that terrible time period in our country; nevertheless, we have a current job market that is hemorrhaging on a financial collapse that could totally devastate our overall economy. So a job seeker is going to have to go the extra mile to get noticed and go above and beyond the call of duty in order to stand out. Needless to say, Ms. Seductive looked at me like I was smoking crack!

Another PTs objective stated: "Seeking to use my warehouse skills to a company where I can grow and be a hard-worker." I advised him to research the specific job title and include the company name. The example I gave him was: "To obtain a warehouse staff position within Nissan Motor Corp of America-with the opportunity for career advancement." You know what his response to me was? "Man Jahi, you wanna go down to the company for me and do what chu talking bout?" I responded with an EMPHATIC "No, that's your job MR. professional job seeker. I'm just giving you some professional pointers on how to effectively market yourself on paper. What you do with this information is totally your prerogative." Yeah, I know, I had to go Bobby Brown on him with the prerogative remark, huh? Oh well! He asked for it and I gave it to him.

The Employment History section is another area where many of our PTs just aren't taking the time and making the effort to research their own work history with accurate dates and marketable duties. One young lady was describing her McDonald's employment experience as such: "Name of company: Macdonals, city: La county; duties: get food, hand out food, gave cusmers food, cleaned tabals and floors, opened place up." Yes! This was a hot mess! To add insult to injury, she was one of our repeat students, aka returning champions, and she was in all of my pre-employment workshops during the first week of JSPC before self-dropping out. Now you guys should know by now that I wouldn't suggest that she incorporate that verbiage! There's no way I would ever advise her to put some hot mess like this on a job application or resume. She was straight tripping! Nonetheless, that's why we conduct these workshops, right? So that we can properly, appropriately, and professionally show our PTs how to effectively market themselves on paper, and in person. Here we go! I pulled her aside and said, "There is no way on God's beautiful earth that you should ever submit some crazy ass stuff like this." I reinstructed her to make the following corrections. Right out of the gate we all grew up around the #1 restaurant franchise globally, established back in 1955 under the collaboration of Ray Kroc and the McDonald's brothers. Now, "Macdonals" could be a knock-off restaurant somewhere over-the-rainbow out there; however, the restaurant that served billions and billions of people around the world is spelled "McDonald's."

Second of all, "La county" could easily be mistaken for the state of Louisiana. The correct way to abbreviate Los Angeles is "L.A." But I suggested to her just spell out the city and abbreviate the state so it'll read, "Los Angeles, CA." She had the audacity to say that I was being too picky and everyone but me would know that "La" county means Los Angeles county.

When we got to the Duties section, I had a Dave Chapelle and Wayne Brady moment when they did that skit where both characters were hanging out having a boy's night on the town. You guys remember that skit? Remember when Wayne's character pulled up on the street corner and summoned his evening ladies over to the SUV where Dave's character was riding in the front passenger seat? As the ladies of the night were handing over $50 and $100 dollar bills to their Pimp Wayne Brady, one of the ladies came up a little short regarding the profit margin expectations of her shift. As Wayne was dangling one of the lonely franklins in his hand, he responded, "Is Wayne Brady gonna have to choke a b----?" Right on cue, Dave's character shouts out, "Run b----, run!" I respectfully apologize to those who HATE the term "b----" and how it's often used in a very derogatory way towards women. Unfortunately, I had one of those RARE "Is Jahi gonna have to choke a b--ch" moments because she was being rude, impatient and totally lacked professional character pertaining to my valiant effort in assisting her with these corrections. Just for the record, I didn't call her a bitch, nor do I call women bitches. Comedy is one of my many therapeutic techniques I regularly use to get me through tough and challenging PT situations. And, this young lady was an EXTREMELY challenging situation to deal with…

The education section is another area where our students quite often leave out key pieces of information. One of our older gentlemen's mistakes consisted of: "Name of high school: Centinella, city/state: La Ca." Dates were missing the years, there was no mention of adult school/community college for a G.E.D. program. I asked him, "Are you referring to Centennial high in Compton, CA?"

He responded, "Yeah."

I said, "Isn't the correct spelling of the high school you attended for two years spelled C-e-n-t-e-n-n-i-a-l?"

His response was, "I don't know!"

I replied by re-emphasizing, "You attended that school for two whole years, saw the humongous sign on the front of the building every day! And you still misspelled the name of your school? Also, the school is in the city of Compton, California not 'La Ca,' wherever 'La Ca' is! Finally, I strongly advised him to let employers know that he's currently attending a G.E.D. program. References are another challenging section for our PTs for the following reasons: First and foremost, they're not using quality/professional references that can provide credibility to the participant. I always recommend that they use one professional, one educational, one volunteerism, just to have balance. Our PTs have used references who were deceased or have disconnected phone numbers or invalid email addresses; they have also used biased family members and ex-significant others who give a negative reference.

One young man used his ex-girlfriend, who totally bad-mouthed him by stating, "He owes me money, and he's a no-good cheating liar," etc. We also remind our PTs to stay in contact with their references periodically and remind them that they're being used as a reference. I'm dumfounded by the amount of inappropriate references our participants use. Other common resume mistakes include: excessive spelling errors; non-usage of multiple symbols such as bullets, underlines, italics, bold, diamonds, and asterisks; failure to use professional terminology/vernacular while describing duties; overall failure to effectively produce a marketable resume.

Interviews are areas where our PTs just need to practice. They need to develop an interview style that can be replicated in every interview they go to. Unfortunately, too many of our PTs fail to take these interviews seriously and practice. This reminds me of when NBA player Allen Iverson, aka "The Answer," was being badgered by the sport's press media for missing practice several seasons ago due to private family matters. One of those sports programs counted the total number of times Iverson mentioned the word practice. The total count was somewhere in the neighborhood of 22 times. Allen kept repeating, "Practice? We talking 'bout practice, not a game, but practice" He also mentioned the fact that he was Philadelphia's franchise player! As I watched that interview, I couldn't help but think back on some other legendary NBA stars like Kareem, Magic, Jordan, Bird, etc. None of them ever trivialized the importance of practice! Magic said that the show-time Lakers practiced harder in practice so that when game time came, Kurt Rambis knew that his role wasn't to come off the bench and start jacking up three point shots. His main role was to body-up in the low post, grab rebounds, and defend the interior paint. I guess that's why Kareem, Magic, Jordan, and Bird collectively have 20 NBA championships, and Iverson is currently playing overseas with 0 rings. Interesting!

CHAPTER 8: *Interviews*

There are so many interview horror stories to share that I can't possibly share them all. However, there are a few that must be told. We instruct our PTs that there is a list of things they must do prior to the interview such as research key pieces of information about the company, bring a portfolio with copies of all professional job search documents such as preprinted master application, several typed resumes formatted for that respective company, writing utensils, scratch paper, two forms of picture identification, California ID/driver's license, certificates, diplomas, degrees, and additional documents relative to the interview. Other invaluable tips we recommend are getting plenty of rest the night/day before, mapping out commute schedule to assure punctuality, avoiding strong odor foods such as garlic and onions, keeping perfumes/colognes to an extreme minimum, dressing for success with conservative, professional colors/outfits, etc. During the interview, we instruct them to thank the interviewer(s) for extending the interview invitation, have a firm handshake, use professional greeting vernacular like "good-morning/afternoon," smile, maintain eye-contact, answer questions directly/effectively, demonstrate good body posture, control nervous habits, thank them at the conclusion of the interview, and submit a thank you card approximately one to two days after the interview. Typically in our interview workshops we go over some basic and commonly asked interview questions like:

1. Could you tell us a little bit about your background?
2. Why do you want to work for our company, business, organization, or corporation?
3. What skills/expertise do you have that would qualify you for this position?
4. Describe a strength you can bring to our organization.
5. Do you have any weaknesses you're working on improving?
6. What are your short-term/long-term goals?
7. Could you share with us some of your leisure hobbies/interests?

8. Describe, explain, or give an example of where you've utilized any of your strengths in a successful employment-related situation.
9. Please share with us one positive experience and one negative experience about a past job.
10. How did you overcome the negative experience?

In answering the opening background question, I've adopted a very clever TEACH acronym from one of my fellow colleagues some years ago. The "T" represents Thanks. Once again, it's about expressing our sincere appreciation/gratitude for even getting the interview opportunity in the most competitive job market of our era. Experience/Education represents the "E." We remind them to highlight total amount of years of self-employment, volunteerism, paid experience they have, or educational accomplishments to date. "A" is for Abilities such as dependable, goal-oriented, productive, team-player, exceptional ability to meet deadlines, efficient multi-tasking of assignments, etc. The "C" stands for Closure. Quite often, PTs talk themselves out of an interview. We recommend that after they've followed the previous T-E-A steps, then an effective C end to this segment is: "If you hire me, I'll be a tremendous asset to this company, business, corporation, or organization." Between company, business, corporation, organization, which terminology should they use, you ask? Depends on how efficiently they did their homework/research on the company. Whichever terminology the company uses as their everyday lingo is the one they wanna use in this situation. The key is to continuously speak the company's language. Finally, the "H" stands for HIRE! What else did you think it stood for? LOL! It's the confidence that says if this company doesn't hire me, I'll take this same interview technique to the next company! Eventually, someone's gotta give me a shot, right? The next question is, "Why do you want to work for our company and not one of our main competitors?" This question is ALL about proper research relative to the company one is interviewing for.

My all-time favorite workshop example is McDonalds. If I were interviewing for a Crew Member position at the Golden Arches, I would also provide company research facts. I'd mention their incredible history, with over 50 years of dominating the restaurant franchise industry, always staying on the cutting edge by introducing new product menus to the forever growing billions and billions of customers served each year. Their advertising/marketing is second to none. One can start out as a Crew Member, and then work their way into management via Burger University, and then position themselves for a possible franchisee stake in the McDonald's family. Ok, this may sound like a 30-second commercial spot for McDonald's; however, it's better than sounding like a second-grader who's trying to explain to his/her teacher why they're crying after injuring him/herself while playing on the monkey bars with his/her fellow classmates–which is how a good number of our PTs typically sound when answering this question. It all goes back to doing proper research on these companies before even stepping foot in the interview room. If I had a penny for every time I heard: "Jahi, that's doing too much" Or, the infamous, "We have to do that research for every interview?" Over the years, I'd be a very wealthy man! It's mind-boggling how so many of our PTs don't want to do that in-depth research on companies prior to their interviews…

Strengths and Areas of Improvement are more about memorization and the ability to recite the information back during the interview. In my classes, I usually give the hip-hop freestyle artist as an example. First and foremost, freestyle rapping in hip-hop music is an art form that not everybody can do, right? They're using the English language in a very creative manner–they rhyme to beats while telling a story. The rappers who can freestyle have an uninterrupted flow to their rap, which doesn't include stuttering, mumbling, loss of concentration/ train of thought. The number one reason why they're good at their respective craft is because they put the time and effort into it via practice. Therefore, I encourage our students to have that freestyle flow mentality when answering this question and the remaining interview questions. They should be able to rattle off strengths such as troubleshooter, efficient, dependable, detailed-oriented, organized, teamplayer, etc. without blinking an eye.

Weaknesses are a little trickier. The trick to answering this question is turning a person's weakness into strength. Turning negatives into positives is the traditionally advised rule of thumb. For instance, being a workaholic is a good weakness to use because it's really a strength and/or an ability. One of our PTs mentioned her mouth as a weakness. When I asked her to elaborate more on that with an example, she began to share a past employment situation where she got into a fist fight with one of her co-workers over a cheating boyfriend scandal. Of course, I reminded her not to share that story during an actual interview setting, due to the negative connotations associated with the story.

The "What are your short/long-term goals?" question is very straightforward and simple. They see themselves advancing, promoting, and/or growing within their company/organization. We remind them not to say, like this one interviewee candidate mentioned to my interview partner and I, dude said he planned on starting a construction company in Mexico. I had to do a double-take at his application/resume because I swore he stated that he was a graduate of our almighty JSPC class. Now, if that's true, he obviously wasn't paying attention during the interview workshop because we don't teach our PTs to give answers like that! We ALWAYS instruct them to say growing/advancing within the company/organization they're interviewing with. Letting the interviewers know that the interviewee would be a good long-term investment for their business is the message that they want to convey. The expression on my interview partner's face was priceless! We both took a "we don't believe this guy just said what we thought he said." Unbelievable! I had to be the one to break the bad news to him and tell him that we would be very concerned about his short/long-term goals to start a construction company in Mexico because he wouldn't be a sensible long-term investment for our welfare-work program. Why even hire the guy when he informed us during the interview that he planned on relocating out of the frickin' country before he could even pass the six-month probationary period, right?

Hobbies/Interests is the fun question with a little trickery to it. Part of the interviewee's homework assignment prior to the interview is to research the non-profit community/charitable work the company is involved in and mention volunteer work that is synonymous with the organization. Let's say the company has a softball team or bowling team. You barely know what a bat looks like and couldn't hit the ball if it were placed on top of a tee-ball cone. However, you can still acknowledge your appreciation for the sport as a fan or just-for-fun willing participant. As for bowling, you slam and noisily drop that smooth round thing into the side gutter ball rail with great consistency. Nevertheless, you enjoy the bowling atmosphere of people having fun! There are ways to share your similar pastime/spare time hobbies/interests in order to further make the likeability factor connection between you and the interviewers. What is a short list of the past-time hobbies I've heard from a good number of our PTs over the years? Smoking weed/drinking alcoholic beverages, having sex, watching pornos, selling bootleg movies/CDs, chop shop work (garages that house stolen cars), gambling, hanging out with "da homies," attending strip clubs, community service (court-ordered), anger management classes, domestic violence classes, mental health appointments, etc. Of course we strongly encourage them not to bring those examples up during the interview. Positive additional examples include: family, non-profit community volunteerism, reading, museums, exercise.

What you appreciated or did not appreciate about previous positions held are also common interview questions. What one appreciated about previous employment is generally an easy response such as customers, co-workers, management, safe working environment, team-oriented atmosphere. What one did not appreciate is a little trickier to answer. The key is to put the blame on the company and not on oneself. For instance: The company didn't have any plans for future growth; they failed to practice state/federal health regulations and standards; company phased out your position or maybe even downsized the department/division. Don't bring up negative things that could possibly make you sound like an "ignorant" dumb-ass like one of our young men. This guy had the audacity to bring up a previous job situation where he was running his illegal drug business within the company. But wait! Ole boy was only working there for a few weeks. Dude wasn't even there long enough to pass probation, much less set up his mini-drug cartel operation. Not to mention he had already served nine years in prison for a drug-trafficking case. Nevertheless,

I encouraged him not to mention his personal *Scarface* scene. At the conclusion of every interview, interviewers always ask, "Do you have any questions for us?" We usually recommend that our PTs ask questions such as, "When do you anticipate making a hiring decision for this position?" "Would you like me to clarify/elaborate on any of my answers to your questions?" "What are some of this company's successes/accomplishments that you are most proud of?"

There have been some interesting interview dress attire outfits worn by our PTs, to say the least. Joan and Melissa Rivers's fashion police would have had a field day with some of the outfits our students have adorned on interviews. Over the years, LACOE has partnered up with many employers in hopes to further assist our PTs in their transition into gainful employment. Hector was one of the main recruiters for one of the largest automotive manufacturing plants in Southern California when he shared with my colleagues and me one of the funniest interview stories I had ever heard…

It was on a hot summer day in 2005–Hector calls the next interviewee candidate from the lobby, when one of our finest PTs, we'll call him Pimpin-Aint-Easy, approached Hector wearing a bright lime-green, yellow pinstripe three-piece suit with matching lime green gators, cherry red tie with a matching hankie, draping gold chains across his upper torso, lime green top hat; gold teeth glistening from his grill. According to Hector, he could barely hold in his surprised facial expression/amazement as he escorted Pimpin-Aint-Easy into the interview room where the other co-interviewers awaited their arrival. As Hector began explaining how this wannabe Pimp-of-the-year could barely speak clear English, Hector said that his other two panel-interview colleagues kept kicking him under the table, in gestures of disbelief; all three could barely hold their utter amazement at this character, rocking the pimp-suit outfit. He said when Pimpin started talking/answering the interview questions, they could barely understand a word coming out of his mouth. Hector said it sounded like he had cotton balls in his mouth with a strong Southern accent. I began to crack-up in laughter! He said this guy was mumbling and fumbling his words so much that all three had to ask if he could repeat himself a couple of times during the first couple of questions of the interview. By this point of Hector telling me the story, I hit the damn floor in at least 10-minutes of hysterically uncontrollable crack-up laughter! I dang near needed an oxygen mask to restore normal breathing. Suffice it to say that they cut the interview short because they couldn't understand a damn word coming out of the dude's mouth.

Wardrobe distractions like Pimpin-Aint-Easy's coming from our PTs are one thing however, when it comes from one of your very beautiful female colleagues, it could take on a totally different meaning. It's autumn season 2005, and one of our outstanding temporary office workers, we'll call her Cinnamon, came into one of our DPSS offices for an early morning permanent intake clerk position interview. Her clerical/administrative skills were impeccable; however, her outfits were a little too sexually provocative for most of us healthy red-blooded heterosexual male colleagues to handle. Each day that she walked through the lobby areas, it was normal to hear inappropriate cat-call heckles such as, "Damn, um-um-um," cackling, and a few whistles as Cinnamon walked past a bunch of male hound-dogs. I have to admit that even the first time we met, my mouth dropped like a nine year-old boy seeing a woman's naked boobs for the first time–quite an unforgettable experience! We worked together as facilitator and office assistant for 6 months before the sexual tension between us became overwhelming. One day Cinnamon had on this see-through blouse with matching tight white see-through pants hugging every curve of her body. The see-through blouse could barely tame her bulging 38DD breasts; her back-side looked like something from a Sir Mix A Lot's "I Like BIG BUTTS" video or something. When she got to my classroom/office, I was totally speechless. It was just before lunch, and her interview for one of the permanent clerk typist positions wasn't scheduled until 1:30 p.m. with the DPSS interview staff. Cinnamon had an absolutely gorgeous music video body. I admit that my mouth was drooling, eyes gawking, adrenaline pumping; I began to speak mumble-jumble. However, I did ask her if she was wearing that particular outfit for that interview. Right on cue, she started slowly turning around so that I could get a slow motion view of every part of that vivaciously enticing body, and she seductively asked what was wrong with her outfit. By this time, I had forgotten all about going to lunch when one of the security guards asked if everything was ok. I told him, "Yeah, we'll be right out in a minute." Why didn't the security guard tell us that he was locking the door for lunch so all we had to do was close it behind us?

Cinnamon asked me again (as I started to notice the smell of Red Door perfume…only one of my ALL TIME favorite women's fragrances), "Jahi, what's wrong with my outfit, honey?"

I asked her, "Is that Red Door perfume you're wearing?"

She said, "Yeah–you like?"

I said, "That is my all time favorite women's perfume!"

She responded by getting closer to me, by stretching out her caramel-complexioned neck on that fine and sexy 5'6" frame; in her hot, sexy and sassy voice she asked, "How does it smell now sweetie?"

All I could do was take a big whiff and sigh, "Um, that smells so good," while using my best suave yet debonair voice impersonation. And, my eyes slowly rolled down her smooth caramel-skinned neck, and down into those pair of soft and tender looking 38DDs, I was temporarily hypnotized by her overall beauty. I then reluctantly mumbled to her that it was time to go to lunch.

When she batted those gorgeous puppy dog soft brown eyes at me and said, "Ok, daddy, only if I can get a good-luck hug from you" I was melting in her hands so fast that I could've done an M&M commercial (melts in your mouth not in your hands). Now, you know by that point I have the biggest erection on earth. As I kept my hands in my pocket trying not to let her see how excited she was getting me, out of nowhere she embraced me in what appeared to be the longest non-church hug ever. As we hugged she immediately smiled and said, "Well, I see I've awakened the sleeping giant." Without even blinking an eye she grabbed my now throbbing hard penis and responded by saying, "Oh my God! What chu got a Louisville slugger down here? Wow! I'm impressed."

I told her "Thank you," and knew we had to get out of there immediately because things were getting way too hot and heavy. Saved by the bell, one of my female colleagues knocked on the door to come in and retrieve her purse from the locked desk. So with the biggest grin/smile, Cinnamon shouted out, "Thanks for wishing me good luck on my interview."

When my colleague overheard that comment she asked Cinnamon, "Oh you have an interview with LACOE?"

Cinnamon replied, "No, it's an intake clerk position with DPSS and Jahi was so instrumental helping me relax and not stress out so much about it." I interrupted both ladies with a Snagglepuss, exit stage left move.

While my colleague was bending over behind the desk to grab her purse, Cinnamon gave me a gentle tap on my butt as she walked passed me and left the room. A few short minutes after Cinnamon's departure, I exited out of the side door and headed out to lunch. Within a few short months after that encounter, Cinnamon called me on my desk phone excited about the fact that she was hired as our permanent site intake clerk. And, she was especially happy about the fact that we would continue working together in the same building. Now my dilemma was whether or not I should date a fellow colleague who works directly in the same office? I've heard of office romances that led to happy relationships before. However, I've also heard of some office romance horror stories. Decisions! Decisions! Well, we will continue on with, "As The World of Cinnamon Turns" a little bit later to see how this potential office romance turns out… Now, back to our regularly scheduled program with the wild & crazy-ass interview outfits rocked by some of our PTs.

One of our other PTs sported a dirty white long-sleeve, see-through shirt with a yellow and black Batman shirt underneath. Now the jacket appeared to have been purchased in the children's section at a local retail store. His pants were black skin tight khakis, with grungy dark grey tennis shoes, and a Mohawk to boot. My first impression when I saw him with that outfit on was Mr. T on crack. Even though he was being interviewed by one of our welfare-friendly employers who were sympathetically understanding to the population at hand, we still had to tell Mr. I-pity-the-fool on crack PT that his interview outfit was totally inappropriate. Remember this: DPSS gives each PT an additional $50 over and above their monthly grant for the sole purpose of purchasing clothes. Now does that mean they can roll-out to Beverly Hills, walk into Versace's clothing store on Rodeo Dr. and go on a shopping spree? Of course not! Or, better yet, in the infamous words of Whitney

Houston, "Hell to the Nah." But, they can go to one of those local thrift stores, Goodwill, Ross, Marshall's, Payless, or DD's, and find some really affordable deals that would appropriately fit the basic professional interview attire we're reinforcing them to adhere to.

Still, there's not a class that goes by where at least half the PTs complain about that $50 not being enough money for them to purchase business casual/dress-for-success attire. I ALWAYS respond by saying how everyone needs to be grateful, appreciative, and thankful for whatever the county is giving them because many states within our country don't have as much welfare love as the state of California.

Unfortunately, between the years 2000 and 2005, the overall conditions of a significant percentage of our PTs began to take a spiral turn downward for the worse due to increases in mental health illness, substance abuse challenges, felony convictions, literacy/educational inadequacies, and homelessness. During this period we continued to lose more and more employers as our go-to job placement partners because they began to step up their efforts in pre-screening qualified vs. non-qualified candidates. What did this mean? Our go-to employers were beginning to perform drug tests, run criminal background checks, and require proof of minimum high school diploma or GED, which subsequently pre-screened our PTs out of employment opportunities. Also, there were a few of our faithful companies that jumped on the welfare-to-work bandwagon back in the mid-1990s that were ready to jump off that bandwagon by 2005. Allow me to share a few true stories from companies that finally said "Adios, welfare-to-work hires" because of all the negative baggage the PTs brought in.

The first business, we'll just say this was one of the leading warehouse manufacturing companies in California. As much as we prepared our PTs for these interviews, too many of them still found ways to screw it up! Upon receiving feedback from the employers during this period, here are a few reasons why we began losing job placement contracts with them: attendance, punctuality, work ethics, and interpersonal relationships with their co-workers. This particular company had been one of our steady go-to employers where we knew we could get job placements.

CHAPTER 9: *Ernie & Luisa*

Our main contact at this company was Big Ernie. Now, Big Ernie was the nicest big teddy bear kind-of-guy that you would ever want to meet. He always had a HUGE smile on his face, was a married family man with three teenage children, and expressed compassion for helping out our welfare-to-work PTs with employment opportunities. However, don't get it twisted for one minute! Ernie had a checkered past! He was once an active gang-member with one of L.A.'s biggest notorious Mexican gangs that had direct Mexican Mafia connections. He served over 20 years of his life in the Youth Authority system and San Quentin Prison for some pretty heinous crimes we don't even have to go into detail about. When I first met Big Ernie, we hit it off immediately! We shared a lot of the same common interests regarding sports, politics, nation-wide/global current event issues, neighborhood drama, our children and women, and we had some real cool man-cave sporting events with the fellas… In any case, Ernie shared some incredibly funny yet unfortunate stories about our PTs that forced him to sever our professional relationship working with this population. Like most of our employers who hung in there with us for a good while before finally cutting ties with us, Ernie and his company were in collaborative partnership by employing our PTs for a good 5 years, until enough became enough! One of our PTs, who Ernie affectionately called Luisa, resembled one of the characters played by Power 106 Air Personality/Actor Big Boy in the 1999 Rob Schneider film, *Deuce Bigalow, Male Gigolo*. He said Luisa got off to a bad start by being 15 minutes late for his swing-shift position on the first day, during the first week on the job.

Ernie pulled Luisa aside after that shift ended and had the hey-man-you're-the-new-kid-on-the-block speech, and showing up late for work, on day number one, during your first week on the job is UNAC-CEPTABLE! Hello! In JSPC, we stress the importance of attendance and punctuality throughout their probationary period. Luisa promised Big Ernie that it wouldn't happen again. Well, by the end of the second week, it happened again.

Ok, I have to give you guys the background of this PT. You see, by day he was a warehouse worker and by night, he was Luisa-the-drag-queen. Ernie didn't know this until little signs started popping up at the worksite and it began affecting the overall work production of the crew. When Luisa was late a second time the following week, Ernie noticed what he thought was lipstick/mascara residue on Luisa's lips/face. Ernie didn't ask him if that was lipstick/mascara or not, until the other warehouse staff members started to inform Ernie about certain inviting behavior from the new guy. For the next two weeks, Luisa was on time; however, his night lifestyle began to manifest itself during the daytime when he accidently dropped these photos of himself dressed up in drag, on the floor, right next to his assigned assembly worksta-tion. Oh, but it gets better you guys…

Ernie began to receive reports from his staff members about Luisa star-ing down at his other male coworkers' urinals as if he was trying to get a sneak peek at his neighbor's family jewels and then singing Gloria Gaynor's "I Will Survive" as he exited the men's restroom. A few of the crew members received invitations to a few West Hollywood events. The final straw came when Luisa was involved in a heated argument with one of the senior warehouse staff members in the staff lounge during their dinner break. Just under Luisa's first month on the job, Ernie called an emergency staff meeting with his entire warehouse production staff crew regarding the brewing tension and the conse-quential heated argument that almost resulted in a fight. The staff was allowed to express their concerns, frustrations, and any uncomfortable feelings that had reached a breaking point with several staff members towards Luisa. Well, you know what happened next right? Damn near the entire staff, minus a few of Luisa's fan base, began to verbally attack his inviting behavior and gay lifestyle. Before another heated argument ensued, Ernie made it mandatory for all staff to attend the company's in-house sexual harassment workshop so that everyone had a clear understanding of what was considered sexual harassment and how certain actions could lead to possible termination from the company.

The senior staff member who got into that very heated argument with Luisa just a few days earlier, stood up, pointed at Luisa and shouted, "That nasty gay bastard needs to kick rocks!" At that moment, all hell broke loose! Luisa went OFF!!! He stood up and used every profanity-laced word in the book as security had to separate the two from going at it for round two. Ernie said Luisa threatened to sue the company by stating, "I will sue this mutha-fucking company and use the settlement money to buy this bitch back and then fire all ya'll bitches...don't fuck with me limp dick mutha-fucka, I'm the wrong queen bitch to fuck with," as he was looking at the senior staff member who made the incendiary remarks while being escorted out of the meeting and subsequently building by security staff. Believe it or not, you guys, all this happened during Luisa's first month on the job. He hadn't even passed the company's standard 90-day probationary period yet. That's Incredible, huh? After having a long conversation with Ernie about this unfortunate incident, he assured me that the reason why his company decided to sever its business relationship with us was due to a series of unfortunate disciplinary actions being taken against mostly our PTs as a result of their unprofessional conduct on the jobsite.

Ernie also re-emphasized how his company embraces multi-cultural diversity, respective of faith/spirituality practices, sexual orientation/lifestyle, and gender friendliness. However, his company would not tolerate the unprofessional behavior that Luisa displayed! On a personal note, Ernie told me that he had no problem working with gay people and that this was just an isolated incident. He went on to share that there were known gay staff members that carried themselves with a high degree of respect, maturity, creativity, and professionalism; a few introduced production ideas that the company had implemented as part of their daily operations. Ditto dude! As I shared my sentiments about the gay community, I said, "To be really honest man, most gay people I've ever met throughout my lifetime thus far have been real cool down-to-earth people! Many are intelligent, creative, success driven; overall, they have friendly personalities that blend into most social circles. And in most communities, unfortunately, just like in every group/culture, there are those Luisa's of the world where it's more about their mental health challenges as opposed to their chosen life-styles… Much respect to our gay workforce!" Then we ended our conversation discussing the details about the upcoming Monday night football fellas hang-out venue location. Not that you my readers really cared about that irrelevant piece of information…LOL!

CHAPTER 10: *A Warm Cup Of Latte*

People come into our lives for many reasons, and during different seasons, but none could ever be more evident of this than when I met a young female employer who made an indelible impact on my personal life as well as my professional life. It was fall of 2005. We were hosting one of our many co-sponsored employer recruitments at one of our sites when I kept feeling these eyes staring at me from a couple of tables over. There were a couple of young hot female recruiters representing this particular staffing agency seeking to recruit our PTs for various light industrial, housekeeping, or warehouse work. These young ladies looked like they should have been part of Vanity Six from Prince's 1980s protégé group, or maybe one of the Spice Girls. The one that caught my eye had an Appolonia meets Vanity look with a nice Scary Spice figure. When I noticed her, I immediately made a bee-line over to their table so I could officially welcome them as employers to our recruitment. Yeah right! I saw a hot-ass sexy young lady that was looking too nice for me not to run my butt over there for proper introductions. As we exchanged pleasurable introductions/greetings, all I could think about was how gorgeous this girl was, and without missing a beat, a few of my ignant (ignorant) ass PTs rudely interrupted our conversation like frickin' first-graders who needed a dang hall pass to use the damn restroom.

As I snapped back from my daze of glaze into her sexy eyes, I politely excused myself to assist the PTs with extra resume copies. But, really I knew those guys were trying to cock-block my action with; let's just call her "Latte"! For the next two hours, I stayed busy assisting our PTs with filling out applications, making copies of various documents, and providing refreshments for our Spice Girls employers. I bent over backwards to make sure Latte received extra-special attention/services. All the hard work paid off because at the end of the recruitment, Latte asked if I could help her transport some of their company literature/materials to her car. I said, "Of course! We're here to provide quality service and assistance to you ladies in order to ensure your positive experience here today, and we hope you'll return for future employer recruitments."

As the ladies burst out in warm giggles, each one hugged the other and headed to their respective cars. The last one hugged Latte, while giving me a "You're a naughty boy" smirk, and headed towards her car. Finally, just me and Latte alone! We both were walking ever so slowly while enjoying one another's conversation. She said it was so sweet of me to cater to her the way I did and that she felt a little guilty that I gave her so much attention. I responded by saying how our PTs treat us like we're their IHOP restaurant servers anyway, so we're used to the service thing. She giggled. We then quickly switched topics to the various challenges of working with this population on a daily basis because just in a short two-hour period, the Spice Girls couldn't believe the things they were seeing/hearing. So for the next 30 minutes, in the parking lot, directly in front of her SUV, Latte and I had the most insightful conversation one could ever have with an employer regarding some of the difficult challenges we face in working with this welfare-to-work population.

Latte said, "Jahi, first of all, I highly commend you and your colleagues for an amazing job you guys are doing in helping them transition into the job market; however, many of them I wouldn't send to our employers for assignments!" She said the first 10 minutes as they were setting up the table, three of our male PTs came over to the ladies talking about "Hey Sexy Ma's, what kind a company is this?" When Latte politely asked them to please give them a second to finish setting up, one of the guys said, "Ah I don't want no job, I just need to grab one of y'all fliers for my teacher." The initial PT who asked what kind a job this is began giving Latte his best Mack-daddy lines about how pretty she was, and how she should give him her number. Latte said she looked at him and his boys with disgust! Then Latte's other Spice Girl colleague politely asked the three gentlemen to give them some set-up time and come back shortly.

When the ladies finally set up their table, the Three Stooges came back to their table talking the same mess, so Latte began to ignore them and directed her attention to greeting and providing information to other PTs who approached the table. She overheard the head Mack-daddy Stooge say, "Aw! She think she too good for us just 'cause we on the county. Whatever Bitch!" Latte said it took every bone in her body to maintain her professionalism, breathe, and continue providing information to our PTs. For the next 45 minutes, she saw PTs dressed in gang-affiliated attire, females in stripper-club gear, huddled conversations where PTs were engaging in profanity, vulgarity, unprofessional conversation topics, some with alcohol and weed aroma on their person; overall, unimpressive behavior. She said that one of our PTs kept coming back to the table every five minutes asking for something different every time. When one of her colleagues finally said, "Sir, do you need anything else?" "No, thank you, I'm just collecting information for my job searches," the PT replied. Latte had me in stitches as she was describing the circus ordeal. She asked me, "How in the world do you deal with these people on a daily basis? And, how on heaven's earth do you help them get jobs?" I said, "Sweetheart, there's no way on God's beautiful earth I can answer this question in one conversation! Therefore, we should meet for lunch one day, and begin our mini-series discussion on how in the world we help these folk find jobs." She responded very favorably by stating that her home office is in San Bernardino County and that she was just down here providing job fair/recruitment role-playing assistance to her staff/colleagues.

As I looked at her job title it read, "Senior Staff Recruiter." I said, "All right, young lady," as I began reading her card aloud as if I were doing a radio spot for KNX news radio. She got a kick out of that and gave me the sexiest smile while flashing those pearly white teeth. Then, as most of you women do when you know you're interested in a guy, you suddenly turn on that cutesy innocent shy role. She gave me that "I like you" stare but I'm gonna give you my shy, Catholic-school-girl handshake goodbye. I said wait a minute! So I gave her my mama would be proud church hug, slipped her card in my Pierre Cardin shirt pocket, opened her door, reminded her to buckle-up and drive safely, and re-emphasized that I would call her soon so we could do lunch. As she was backing up she smiled and said, "Goodbye, Mr. Specialist," while displaying that girlish blush. I immediately replied, "Take care, Ms. Senior Staff Recruiter," as I got the final laugh out of her.

Now, I know that the golden traditional dating rule is that you don't call your dating interest the same day you meet them! You should always wait a few days so you don't appear overly desperate. And at the time I was dating my on-again-off-again young lady Ménage from Long Beach, so I waited a full week to call Latte. It must have been perfect timing because she was very happy to hear my voice. It was on a Thursday morning, I dialed her number, and she picked up the phone, "Thank you for calling....speaking." I said, "Good morning, Ms. Senior Staff Recruiter, this is Mr. Specialist from last week's recruitment." She responded like someone who hadn't spoken to their favorite friend in a long time, "Hey stranger, how are you? I was wondering if you were going to call me or not." "Yeah, I didn't want to impose on your busy schedule." Subsequently, we talked for awhile, and then agreed to touch bases to schedule lunch soon. That following Monday came, and I was greeted with a pleasant but dangerous surprise! Cinnamon walked into my office with a cheerful, "Good morning, Mr. Kweli. How was your weekend?" I said, "It was nice. What about yours? So what brings you down here?" I asked her. "It's my first day here at this site; they're showing me paperwork, the check-in process, and additional procedures." I was surprised to see her here so fast; she was looking very nice–wearing a tight black skirt showing every curve of her curvaceous figure. And she had on a red blouse with those breasts safely secured in her bra. I knew nothing could happen between us at that moment because we had to call the a.m. PTs inside the classroom.

Throughout the class session, she must've walked in and out of my classroom several times asking if I needed anything. Each time she walked into the room, she drew cackling responses from several male PTs. Finally, one of the PTs asked, "Dang Jahi, how do you work here when you have a fine ass distraction like that?" I replied by saying, "Nah, we keep it professional around here." At the conclusion of the morning class, all of the PTs had exited the class when Cinnamon confidently walked into the classroom shut the door and ran up to me and gave me the longest bear hug, planted a soft kiss on my cheek and said, "I missed you." We disembarked from our warm embrace, followed by her asking me what I was eating for lunch. "I'm not sure, Maybe Japanese today–you?" She brought lunch so she was headed to the break-room to eat. The day ended on a decent note. However, the next three days were like a countdown to a main event fight. Every outfit Cinnamon wore was sexier than the previous. We engaged in daily county business paperwork/procedures while the sexual tension was growing by leaps and bounds.

Now after about a month of phone calls, text messages, and business travel, Latte and I finally set a lunch date. It's a November Latte Thursday morning, and I went through my daily morning ritual while thinking about my lunch date with Ms. Senior Recruiter. I gave her an early morning reminder call, we confirmed our meeting restaurant, and continued on with the workshop business. Time to roll! As the lunch hour approached, I grabbed my blazer, walked past Cinnamon and told her, "I'm off to lunch and won't be back for the rest of the day."

She replied, "Have fun with that hoochie you going to lunch with!"

I said, "What hoochie?" thinking, *did I tell Cinnamon about Latte? That's an ultimate man-card suspension if I did. Nah! It's just a lucky guess. Or is it?* I said, "Nah, I got an advanced time-off approval from my supervisor over a month ago."

"So who you going to lunch with then?" she asked.

"Lunch meeting with an employer," I answered in a calm, cool, and collected manner. "Ok, Mommy, should I be back home before the street lights come on?" With a smirkish grin on my face, I gave her a smile and a smooth wink. She responded by bowing her head in an embarrassed gesture, and I couldn't get out of the building fast enough. Next, I acknowledged 10 of my fellow colleagues with variations of hello greetings as I passed by each of their cubicles and headed towards the parking structure. The bright sunshine beamed down on my head, I unlocked the car door, popped in one of my favorite Isley brothers CD and mashed out. The drive to the city of Claremont was pretty good–no damn traffic! I exited off the 10 freeway to our agreed upon Thai food restaurant place, swooped into the parking lot, jumped out of the car like I was detective Ricardo Tubbs from Miami Vice–minus the fly-ass Ferrari Testarossa, of course! Upon entering the restaurant, I hear this "Good afternoon, sir," from behind. It was Latte coming from the ladies' room. We embraced each other very firmly, then the host escorted us to a table seating, as I followed behind Latte watching every switch of that sexy derriere. She was wearing a perfectly fitted cream silk blouse, with a beige pants power-suit outfit, matching beige shoes to boot, an earth-tone print scarf and an authentic Gucci purse securely fastened over her left shoulder. Her ensemble was definitely not purchased at JC Penney; you could tell that she shopped at one of those high-end stores. Meanwhile, I rocked my normal Men's Warehouse wool navy blue corporate suit with a flashy but confident tie and black Bostonians from Macy's. After complimenting one another on our appearances she asked, "What is that delicious cologne you're wearing?"

I answered in my best Pepe le Pew impersonation, "It is a French Cologne called Steel Mod."

"Really," she replied, "I was a men's Obsession fan, but now I have a new number one men's cologne. I didn't want us to stop hugging because you smelled so good."

"Oh, really!" I responded by saying, "Well let's pick back up where we left off after lunch," garnering a pleasant laugh from her soft brown Clinique lips. We then proceeded with our small-talk about how the day had been progressing thus far as we both scanned the menu. The server came and inquired about drinks. She ordered a glass of water with lemon and a small Thai tea with no cream. I immediately responded, "Ditto! I'll have the same." The server asked if we needed a minute to decide on our selection.

"No, I'm ready if you are?" asked Latte.

"Yes, I am," as I deferred to Latte to order first, so she ordered the Pad Thai with chicken, and I followed with ordering Pad Thai with tofu and no egg.

"Vegetarian?" she asked. as the server left our table.

"Yes, I am!"

"How long?"

"About 12 years now since my college days."

"Really!" with an impressed look on her face. "I was a vegetarian for awhile during my freshmen year in college."

"Oh!" I replied. "Which college did you attend?"

"Berkeley," with a proud response on her face. "Which college did you attend?"

"Cal State Fullerton."

"Oh wow, I'm thinking about entering their graduate business program."

"Really," I responded. "You can't go wrong with one of the top business schools in the country."

"Yeah! Their business program is well-respected nationally, and this will look good on my resume as I further climb our company corporate ladder," she replied. "Enough about me Mr. Specialist, I wanna hear more about you."

"What would you like to know?"

"How long have you been with LACOE?"

"10 years going on 25 years it seems like sometimes…"

"Do you love what you do?"

"I enjoy the facilitation/presentation of the workshops the MOST; however, it still frustrates me when I see grown, able-bodied adults not even make a sincere effort regarding their job searches, especially when I truly believe in my heart-of-hearts that 100% of them can do SOMETHING to earn a legal legitimate income. Way too many of them have so much wasted/un-used talents and skill-sets that it's so disheartening to stomach…"

"I can't tell by looking at your demeanor because you seem to be so positive and really enthusiastic about what you do," she said.

"Well, thank you for those warm compliments! I'm naturally a very positive person with a ton of energy/enthusiasm about the possibilities of my future. All I attempt to do in these workshops is convey the message of Empowerment! We present them with invaluable tips, professional tools, effective techniques and marketable trade secrets to move from welfare-to-work; however, they have to look in the mirror and wanna build a bigger, better, brighter future by embracing their God-given talents, implementing those talents by setting short-term/long-term employment/career goals, and overall, for them to desire something greater than this welfare system."

"How do they respond to your facilitation style?"

"The majority of my thousands of workshop evaluations over the years I've received have/had good to excellent marks. I received thousands of written comments about my facilitation workshops, and the PTs include evaluation language such as: positive experience, informational, inspirational, motivational, knowledgeable, professional, great-sense of humor, excellent facilitator, and additional flattering comments."

"That must make you feel good."

"It does. I can't lie about that! Their remarks are fuel to my longevity tank in this profession. It lets me know that I'm on the right track with my presentation style and teaching philosophy."

"Wow! That's powerful," she replied.

"Our PTs have all the power in the world to change the complexion and the direction of their future. Unfortunately, a significant percentage of them choose to bathe in the toxic pool of a powerless state of 'oh pity me' being, while short-circuiting their opportunities for a powerful future."

"You sound like Les Brown or Tony Robbins!" she stated.

"Thank you," I replied! "They are two of my favorite motivational speakers, Anthony Robbins being my favorite." A silence brewed for a few seconds…

"Do you have any favorite female motivational speakers?" she asked.

"Oh, that's easy," I responded. "Without a doubt, it's Suze Orman!"

With a huge Kool-Aid smile on her face, she enthusiastically responded, "Oh my God I love her!"

"She's awesome huh?" I interjected.

"Yes! She is," as Latte's eyes glistened like a five year-old girl being awakened by Santa Claus on Christmas Eve, taken up the chimney onto the rooftop, where Rudolph and the other reindeers await, Saint Nick securely fastening the little girl onto the sled while they all depart on a magical journey to the North Pole. Silence brewed once again for what seemed like an eternity as we both gazed into each other's eyes. The server brought our plates over to the table. "Here we are!" snapping us both out of our pleasant trances.

As we began eating our food, the conversation quickly shifted to past/current dating relationships. Earlier that year, she ended a five-year relationship, which included a brief engagement, and culminated in a break-up. I informed her about my eight year-old son from a previous marriage, and I paused to see her body language/reaction to what I just said. Without missing a beat, she said, "Yeah, my parents divorced when I was eight and I turned out fine."

"Yes! You certainly have," I interjected.

"I'm sure your son will turn out just fine because he has such an amazing Dad!"

I dang near choked on my food, and responded with a very sincere, "Thank you very much sweetheart, that means so much for you to say that not even really knowing me very well!"

"I feel you have a genuine spirit," she said. "And I'm a pretty good judge of character! It's a natural God-given gift I've always had."

"Well, I think you are an amazingly intelligent, gorgeously beautiful, and deservingly successful young 21st century career woman with a bright future ahead."

"Awe! Thank you very much, Mr. Handsome."

We both remembered when our server asked if we needed anything else, and she even came back a few times to check on us; however, time stood still as we were intently engaged in an over two-hour lunch conversation. As she checked her Gucci watch, and I checked my Rolex knock-off special from a Venice beach vendor, she sadly said, "I have to be getting back to the office now."

I told her, "Aw! I don't want you to go!"

In an almost sad puppy dog pouting gesture, she responded, "I know, I don't want this lunch to end. However, I do need to get back to the office."

I replied in an understanding fashion, "Yeah, we need to get you back." I paid the bill, and then we headed out to the parking lot. As we approached her champagne-colored 2004 Lexus SUV, she disarmed her alarm, and we stood about a foot away from the driver's side, within kissing distance from each other's lips. I wanted to kiss this girl so bad! Nevertheless, I played the cool gentlemen role and gave her a long church hug, which turned into a brief sinner's grind. She couldn't release me from our bear hug embrace because she kept admiring my Steel Mod cologne. Of course, I hammed it up even more by extending my neck towards her nose while saying, "Take your time and get a good whiff of France's finest fragrance for men."

She closed her eyes and let out three extremely seductive, "um, um, um" moans of "ooh that smells so good, you're driving me crazy now!" she said. By this time, I was getting very aroused and was most definitely enjoying the moment. We stood for a few more seconds gazing into one another's eyes, when she gave me a final compliment that warmed my heart. As she got into her car, started the engine, and fastened her seat-belt, she said, "Call me, sexy eyes, so we can go out soon!"

"Ok gorgeous, drive safely," I said.

"Bye!" she said as she drove off.

It's Friday morning, and I didn't sleep a wink. I was thinking about Latte the entire night. I got up out of bed and put on my casual Friday gear, executed my normal morning routine, hit the garage and mashed out to work. Traffic on the 710 freeway was normal morning rush hour bullshit, but I didn't care because I had Latte on my mind. I swooped into our employee parking structure, exited my Bronze Oldsmobile Alero listening to R. Kelly's "12 play," and entered the building. Next, I walked past my usual partners-in-crime colleagues, gave my weekly Friday greetings, and headed straight to my office. Not a minute after I was about to sit down, Cinnamon walks in, "Good morning, Daddy. How was the rest of your day yesterday?"

"Good, and yours?" I replied. Of course, Cinnamon was looking very nice, but I had Latte on my mind! A few hours later after completing my facilitation class, I gave Latte a call. Ring!

"Thank you for calling… this is… T.G.I.F."

As I also gave her my normal Friday greeting, she responded with an excited, "Hi handsome, how are you?"

"Doing well, gorgeous, and you?"

"Busy per usual, got a few meetings on tap for the day, but then I'm hitting the spa."

"Spa? Which one do you go to?"

"Glen Ivy," she answered. "Wanna go?"

"Ooh! That sounds so good, but I gotta pick up my little man after work."

"That's ok," she replied, "you're such a responsible dad, that's so honorable!"

"Awe! Thank you…I'm just trying to be the best dad for my little dude!"

"Awe! That's so cool," she responded. "Hey! Let's touch bases in a few weeks when I get back from vacation, and maybe we could plan to go dancing? I haven't been dancing in a while, so I was thinking we should go."

Without even hesitating to take a breath I said, "Most definitely yes!" Little does she know that I absolutely love to dance! Get me on the dance floor and I turn into a possessed dancing machine.

Jokingly she asked, "Now you don't have two left feet, do you?"

With a modest chuckle I said, "Well if I do, you can be my dance instructor for the evening!" Upon rattling off a few more funnies, Latte began to crack up hysterically! I could imagine her on the floor next to her desk keeled over trying to catch her breath!

After what seemed like five straight minutes of hysterical laughter, she said, "Look–my sides can't take any more laughter!" After catching her breath, we ended the conversation on a TTYL note. The rest of my afternoon consisted of paperwork and a division-wide training meeting.

Unfortunately, for years leading up to this point, there had been a growing divide between frontline staff and middle-management. In every work environment family, there are always going to be challenges, conflicts, and disagreements. Nonetheless, it takes true team spirit to be able to work through those obstacles for the overall good of the organization progressively moving forward. An example of this would be my own GAIN division. Our division middle-managers held the official job title of Job Developers for 13 years until they moved forward to have the job specification codes changed back in 2006. Ok, so why the sudden job spec move? Well, correct me if I'm wrong, but if a person holds the job title of "Job Developer," isn't that person supposed to develop jobs? I first realized this wasn't happening back in 1996.

I was sitting in a staff meeting and our frontline staff's professionalism was being challenged due to low job placement rates, and our division job developers were demanding that the frontline staff step up job development activities for our PTs. Several sites were hemorrhaging on low job placements, and we desperately needed the aggressive execution of job development by our Job Developers. Surprisingly, most of them were not job developing at all, nor were they even concerned about making a concerted effort to job develop as a team. Now, at that particular time in our division, we desperately needed them to step up, do their jobs, and develop jobs for our PTs. However, they weren't! Therefore, when I asked the question, "Why aren't you Job Developers developing jobs for our sites?" The response I got blew my mind!

One of our Job Developers said, "Well, Jahi, Job Developer is just a job title we have, but we don't really job develop!" I had a Scooby Doo moment (with his signature sound effects).

I responded by saying, "That makes no sense! That's like a Cashier who doesn't want to operate a cash register, a Chef who doesn't want to touch food, or a Lifeguard who doesn't want to jump into the water! If one holds the job title of Job Developer, they need to develop jobs–PERIOD!" I went on to further add that job development is a key component in assisting our PTs with gainful employment. Fortunately, years later, we were able to work out our internal differences and provide quality job development efforts for the overall employment success of our PTs. Nevertheless, I was very fortunate to have job developed Lady Latte and her company, which paid HUGE dividends regarding job placement opportunities for our PTs... And, on a personal note, it gave me an opportunity to get to know Latte a little better...

CHAPTER 11: *A refill cup of Hot Latte*

In early December 2005, Latte was back from vacation, and it was time to get our boogie on. We arranged to meet up at this cozy little older-crowd adult night-club in San Bernardino County. Finally, an evening with Latte! On a clear, cool Saturday night, I hopped on the 10 freeway and headed east. The drive was a peaceful one as I had Latte on my mind and the smooth sounds of the Stylistics to keep me company. I got off at the designated exit and pulled into a parking lot full of nice cars and well dressed people. Admittedly, I felt a little out of place with all those expensive cars surrounding my frugal Oldsmobile Alero. However, I'm from Gardena, the entertainment capital of south bay L.A. County, where we embrace fun! I called Latte on my cell phone and she picked up with super loud music playing in the background. The time read 9:45pm as I flipped my phone back in its case. Before I could go through the usual pat down by a big-ass Sumo wrestler working security, Latte comes to the front of the line and yells, "Big T, he's with me, let him through." At that moment I felt like a celebrity or something. Latte was looking absolutely stunning! Hair did, nails done, make-up perfectly laid, dressed to kill in a super-tight black mini-skirt outfit, looking like Beyoncé backstage at an awards show. We greeted each other with a big hug, and complimented one another on our outfits. Even though I was rocking my downtown L.A. garment district evening gear, she admired my black snakeskin shoes, along with my dark blue rayon shirt and black wool pants. But guess what she really liked? You guessed it: my Steel Mod. She held my hand as we headed for the private reserved booth. Almost immediately as we sat down, the waitress asked us for our drink order. Latte ordered a Cadillac Margarita, which is my second favorite smooth drink behind Long Island Iced Tea. I responded, "Make that two Cadillac's, please!" Then I asked her with an impressive nodding of the head, "I see you have some celebrity star pull here."

"Yeah, it's one of my regular spots."

"Wow, I feel so honored that you brought me to one of your regular spots so early in our dating relationship."

"You should because I don't do this for any ole guy! I have a real comfortable feeling about you." For the next 30 minutes we discussed the events of the week, our jobs, and other current events topics as we pounded two quick Cadillac Margarita rounds. Then suddenly, the D.J. began to play some popular dance hits from the 1980s, when out of nowhere she abruptly grabbed my hand and dragged me onto the dance floor. As Cameo's "Just Like Candy" was playing, I gave her some of my smooth warm-up body boogie moves first as a teaser and appetizer of what would soon follow. Halfway through Candy, she pulls my head down and whispered, "You have some sexy hip movements!"

"Thank you, you're real smooth yourself," reciprocating the compliment. "This is just the appetizer right here, baby girl, because if the D.J keeps bumping like this, it's about to get funky up in here." Staring up at me with those sexy hazel eyes, she had the biggest grin as we boogied for the next hour straight, before she needed to take a breather. When we headed back to the table, we ordered another round of Cadillac's. My general philosophy when drinking is to stop at two drinks and dance the rest of the night until I'm safe enough to drive. Therefore, I told her that this would be my last drink tonight because I really don't like to drink and drive. She concurred, and we continued chatting for the next 45 minutes until the D.J. slowed it down by playing the Isley Brothers "For the Love of You." We both looked at each other and headed straight to the dance floor. We cha-cha'd our asses off as we gave each other one seductive look after another. Right after that song, he merged into Switch's "I Call Your Name," as we danced closer together doing variations of dirty dancing meets freaking. Then I nearly slapped the D.J. when he put on Luther Vandross's "Superstar"! I grabbed Latte like I was Teddy Pendergrass telling her to turn off the lights. I embraced my crotch firmly against her vajayjay, making sure it had no escape, as I positioned my right leg in between her legs, embraced her 36C cups into my chest, while gently rubbing her back periodically. As we began to slow dance, she rested her head against my chest, and as our body temperatures rose to heat wave levels, we consensually allowed our lower bodies to massage, grind, and basically dry hump each other for the duration of a few slow songs. After that sensual workout on the dance floor, we went back to the table and chilled for another 30-45 minutes before hitting the dance floor until shortly past 1:30 am. Then she said, "Let's go!" We went back to the table, paid the tab, and headed out the door. I thought I was going to give her a goodnight hug and maybe a nice long kiss, and then head back home. However, Latte had other plans in mind.

Upon saying her good-byes to both staff and security, we walked outside into the freezing-ass San Bernardino County cold. Unexpectedly, she surprised me by inviting me over to her house for a night-cap. I accepted, of course! We then both jumped into our respective vehicles as she instructed me to follow close behind her. Now most people who know me very well know that I rarely go over 80 miles per hour, because I don't like getting unnecessary speeding tickets, even if I'm heading to Vegas. Nevertheless, this girl had us flying down the 215 freeway like we were in a NASCAR-sponsored event. She had to have been going well over 100 miles per hour because I was doing 90 easily. All I could think of was that we were gonna get pulled over for speeding. It had been hours since drinking the first couple Cadillac's, and all that dancing must've burned off most of the alcohol content in my body, because I didn't feel buzzed at all… Nonetheless, I was still a little nervous about potentially getting pulled over and possibly going through a sobriety roadside test. I called her on my cell phone and asked if she could please slow down a bit, just in case one of us gets pulled over. She apologetically agreed to slow down to a cool 75 mph.

We get to her upscale neighborhood borderline city of Upland and Rancho Cucamonga. As we approached her huge driveway, she had me park in front of her garage while she pulled her car inside. After exiting our cars, we cut through her garage into the laundry area, passed by both the kitchen and living room, and she led me straight upstairs to the bedroom. As we ascended up the spiral staircase, I couldn't help but compliment her on how beautiful her home was. She responded with an appreciative, "Thank you very much."

When we got to the extraordinarily large master bedroom, my mouth dropped as I blurted, "Oh my God, this is how Senior Advisors for your company are living? Man, I'm IMPRESSED!"

With a shy laugh, she said, "Have a seat, and make yourself at home while I get us some refreshments." I plopped down on what felt like a very expensive mini-sofa from one of those high-end Beverly Hills furniture stores. She put on a Marvin Gaye CD, entered the bathroom for a brief five minutes, and then summoned me inside... As I entered her huge bathroom, separated by his/her sinks, I was pleasantly received by red/purple softly dimmed lights, beige soft rugs with matching beige towels hanging on the towel bar, steam coming out of the dual sunken bath/hot tub Jacuzzi, fresh cold fruit laid out on the outskirts of the hot tub, and her sexy voice telling me to jump in! I must've undressed in about 1.5 seconds! Subsequently, the next few hours were one of the most erotic, exotic, and intimately romantic evenings of my life. With a crescendo of silky moans, sensual groans, high-pitched tones, we passionately explored each other's bodies until the break of dawn.

The feel of the morning atmosphere had awakened me to Latte sleeping on my chest so peacefully, and when she finally awakened, Latte and I had a very insightful pillow-talk conversation. It turned out that she was dating an NBA athlete, and who was in turn providing her that beautiful home to live in, with all expenses paid for, as long as she maintained an open-ended intimate relationship with him. We discussed several topics, along with my concerns about dating her under the current conditions/circumstances.

"How long have you dated Mr. NBA?"

"Five years," she responded. "Dating him is going to afford me the opportunity to have connections in the league as I pursue a career in sports medicine... That's what I'm truly passionate about! What are you truly passionate about, Babe?" she asked me.

"I enjoy facilitating JSPC workshops; however, I'm truly passionate about motivational speaking!"

"Well! Then you should passionately pursue what you're passionate about," she replied."

"Yeah! You are absolutely right!"

She then reminded me of how we all have an ultimate purpose in life, and that once we find that ultimate purpose, and combine it with a fiery passion to attain it, then nothing can stop us from achieving what we were put on this earth to do! We continued with our very inspirational career discussion until it was time for me to leave. The drive home got me thinking about a career as a Motivational Speaker. I couldn't help but to think about some of my favorites such as Suze Orman, Les Brown, Joel Olsten, and my all-time favorite, Tony Robbins. From that moment on, I decided to treat every workshop as if I were a world-renowned professional motivational speaker. And I would inspire all of our PTs to aspire to follow their dreams, pursue their passions, and fulfill their ultimate purpose in life. Little did I know that an evening of passion with Latte would inspire me to passionately pursue my ultimate career passion while inspiring others.

The rest of my Sunday consisted of my usual routine: Islands restaurant where I ordered my usual vegetarian burger meal, hung out with a few friends, watched a few sports games, and we discussed current events. I also spoke to my maternal grandmother Nana via phone from Hartford, CT, and I had my weekly phone conversation with my mom. Now, my mother had just moved to New Mexico where the lifestyle is at a much slower pace than the hustle and bustle of Los Angeles, CA. I shared with Moms about my new dating partner and her normal "just be careful" motherly advice followed the end of our conversation. For the next year, Latte and I dated on a fairly regular basis, making the obvious adjustments during the NBA off-season. Little did she know, I was falling in love with her, but I knew that she was still emotionally/financially attached to a guy who I couldn't financially compete with! It was frustrating, yet, it was the reality I signed up for and had to deal with… Outside of our dating relationship, Latte's agency was hiring a good number of our PTs for the next year.

By the summer of 2006, my life was pretty routinely scheduled. Latte and I were happily dating while Cinnamon and I decided to just focus on providing quality services for our PTs and not pursue an intimate dating relationship. In most companies and businesses, your co-workers become like a second family due to the amount of time spent together. And then the miraculous epiphany hit me like a ton of bricks! Latte was brought into my life to make sure that I would fulfill my destiny! That ultimate purpose we all have on this earth! She was my inspirational guardian angel. And my heavenly reminder that I have a greater calling and mission. Don't we all have a unique calling, a significant mission, and an ultimate purpose in life? Imagine if Picasso or Rembrandt never stroked a portrait canvas using a paint brush! What if Handel, Chopin, or Beethoven never composed a symphony! Where would America be without the Abolitionist Movement, Women's Movement, and Civil Rights Movement? What if Muhammad Ali never graced the boxing world with his "I'm the Greatest of All Times" mesmerizing boxing skills? How many young inner-city kids were and are inspired because Venus and Serena Williams picked up tennis racquets at an early age? Picture a Michael Buffer boxing match announcement and he fails to say "Let's get ready to…" Or a professional sporting event underway without the singing of the "Star Spangled Banner." Imagine a Phil Collins concert without him performing "In The Air Tonight" or "Sussudio," Celine Dion leaving out "My Heart Will Go On," Prince not performing "Purple Rain," "Good Times" without J.J., Soul Train without the soul train line…. These are historically legendary figures that have/are passionately pursued/pursuing their calling, and they have left indelible trademarks on humanity.

CHAPTER 12: *It feels like Vegas*

One of the great intangibles about sub-contracting under DPSS and providing JSPC services to the many sites throughout Los Angeles County are the fringe entertainment benefits and perks that come along with it. None could ever be more of a perfect example than the DPSS site that never sleeps. It's now spring of 2007, and I've transferred to a site that is simply UNBELIEVABLE! I affectionately compare this site to "Las Vegas- because the type of fun we had there was amazingly entertaining! Don't get me wrong, though! We worked very hard each and every day; however, we learned how to really enjoy and fully embrace the many district activities that were designed to increase team spirit and unity amongst district staff members. My first day as I pulled up into the parking structure, I was greeted by security staff who escorted me into the building via a secured side staff entrance/exit. I was then warmly greeted by one of the DPSS staff who graciously gave me a guided tour of the entire building while introducing me to all of my new site colleagues. The entire district building holds over 450 staff, and I'm sure I met at least 350 of them the first day alone. I have to admit that it was a bit overwhelming; however, each one of them welcomed me with such open arms and overall positive energy that I couldn't help but to be very encouraged about working side-by-side with them on a daily basis.

By week's end, I met the site director and members of the activities committee. Each DPSS staff reminded me to encourage our PTs to take full advantage of the services available to them. The following week I conducted orientation motivation and a GSW from DPSS came in at the end of the class to inform our PTs about all the available services offered to them. She reminded them that there is substance abuse and mental health counseling, homeless housing assistance, homeless court (pay-off of up to thousands of dollars of unpaid misdemeanor ticket citations), domestic violence services, expungement workshops. Not surprisingly, the service that most of the PTs inquired about was the homeless court because of the possibility of dismissing thousands of dollars of unpaid ticket citations; however, the other services weren't requested. After a few months of observing how so many of our PTs were not taking advantage of the services available to them, I had to find out why. I decided to conduct my own unofficial in-house six-month research project on this matter by interviewing the majority of the EWs, GSWs, and Mental Health staff. It was eye-opening to say the least. The Mental Health staff informed me that if a PT doesn't request mental health and substance abuse services, they were unable to force them or make it mandatory that the PTs receive those complimentary services available to them. Think about it! A PT enters JSPC, and we identify him/her as a mentally challenged or–the crowd favorite–substance abuse challenged. Now, if they refuse mental health and/or substance abuse services, our JSPC suffers tremendously because we're at a severe disadvantage in assisting them with obtaining gainful employment inside of three weeks. Meaning, if an identified pot-head or crack-head enters our program, which occurs on a very regular basis, we can't make it mandatory that Mary Pot-head Jane, Johnny Crack-head, or Willie Weed-head receive the treatment services they desperately need.

So how does this affect job placement percentages? Well, at the conclusion of my six-month unofficial private in-house research investigation, comparing over 36 classes, and over a thousand PT enters, the break-down of what was truly going on was startling. My private, unofficial in-house research was comprised of class roster enrollment forms, information sheets completed by PTs, employment profiles which gather barriers to employment information, class poll feedback from PTs, and interviews from my fellow colleagues regarding their class experiences, along with my own classroom experience observations. Needless to say, I retrieved some very accurate unofficial research information straight from the heart of the sources.

What my unofficial studies concluded was that, on average, 38% of the PTs who entered our JSPC program during that period had a felony or multiple felony convictions on their records which limited their job searches to only the felony-friendly companies, which will re-visit very shortly. Next, another 42% had a substance challenge, primarily marijuana. Now these were averages, of course. Some classes had higher percentages but none fell under the 38% and 42% respective find-ings. That's about 80% of the internal case studies. The mental health cases were much more difficult to measure because most of our PTs didn't acknowledge on paper nor verbally express their mental health challenges; each individual facilitator had to make that professional recommendation. That's approximately 80% of our PTs with a felony criminal conviction background and/or substance abuse challenge(s). Therefore, in some of our JSPC classes, between 65-75% of the PTs would obtain short term temporary job assignments via a staffing agency. Unfortunately, most of those assignments never turned into permanent job placements, for various reasons, and subsequently, our PTs were right back at square number one, repeating our JSPC classes all over again–inside of six months. This has been a vicious cycle I've witnessed over the years.

Now once again, there are numerous reasons why PTs don't complete the full term of temp-to-perm staffing agency assignments, many of which we've already discussed. Nevertheless, it always goes back to the PTs' inability or ability to maintain employment. When I observed how many PTs weren't passing probation nor completing their respec-tive job assignments, I realized that their barriers to employment was their Achilles' heel and that job retention was a major deficit. Some of the things I really admire about the "Twelve Steps Program" are: acknowledging an addiction, taking ownership and responsibility for the addiction, and utilizing the support system provided in order to implement a healthier life style, and by not allowing the addic-tion to take control over their lives. It's all about the addict taking back positive control of his/her life and moving forward in a healthier manner. Welfare-to-work is about the PT taking back positive control of their lives via employment, or through other means of earning a legal legitimate living, and all while releasing the shackles of the EBT card and moving forward with their lives. I've seen a segment of our PTs become addicted to that EBT card like a wino to alcohol, a crack-head to crack, a gambler to a casino, a butt-head to cigarettes, etc. It's almost like some sort of a powerful spell cast upon the recipient. This has become a real serious welfare-to-work addiction. The following is behavior I've witnessed when PTs felt threatened about their benefits being cut: crying, yelling/aggressive outburst, cursing, verbal threats towards staff, tossing of classroom furniture, and additional behaviors of angry addicts. Doesn't this sound like an addict going through withdrawal? For many, the EBT card has become their addiction! Here's an example of the EBT addiction and one of the behavioral effects it has on our PTs.

It was late summer of 2007 when one of our desperate PTs attempted to offer me sex in exchange for not dropping her. In order for our students to successfully complete the JSPC program with a certificate of completion, they must submit a three-page master application, typed resume, and a specified amount of job searches on their employer contact sheets, which we'll get into later on in this book. Now, I give all of my PTs daily verbal reminders of the assignments needed in order to complete the program. They're provided typed resume assistance, for those who request it, and they're given two full weeks to complete their job searches. On day 15, which is the final day of their three-week JSPC experience, it is too late to submit assignments after a certain deadline time because we have to enter their final completion status into our computer mapping system and prepare for the new classes that following Monday. Why did this young lady start pleading and begging me not to drop her like a crack-head begging for another hit?

All of my colleagues who've worked with me know very well how I give all of our PTs daily reminders and warnings and offer assistance regarding typed resumes; however, some always wait until the last day. It was late in the day, just a few minutes before my 4:30 departure time. My colleague had just departed for the day, and I was the only staff member left in the classroom. Out of nowhere, one of my closing class female students came busting through the door, breathing out of control, while almost having a panic attack. Now, for two weeks I'd given this young lady daily verbal reminders about staying on top of the job searches, and I even offered to help type her resume up. What did she do for a two-week job search period? She completed about half of what she was supposed to do in order to complete the program. So now Miss Betty Boop Figure comes into my classroom.

"Hi Jahi, I tried calling your number but you didn't answer."

"Yeah, I just came back from the restroom and I'm about to leave in a few minutes."

"Well, I wanted to turn in my last job searches and ask if you can let me turn in my resume on Monday."

"It's too late now. We've entered the final stats into the computer and closed you guys out already."

"Oh no, please Jahi, I have my searches right here…"

As I looked at her searches, I told her, "Young Lady, these are totally incomplete, and you never corrected the red marks from the previous searches. And I gave you plenty of opportunities to turn in your resume, even offering assistance…"

"I know, Jahi, I screwed up bad. But please don't drop me. My worker said they'll cut my benefits If I don't complete."

"Then that should've given you motivation and determination to submit the mandatory assignments/searches needed in order to complete the program."

"I'm so sorry, Jahi, what can I do to make it up? I apologize…"

"Yeah, but it's too late now, and I'm about to get my keys and get up out of here."

"Please, Jahi, I'll do anything you ask. Do you need any special favors?"

"Do I need any special favors?"

"Yeah, like wash your car?"

"No I'm good, got my own spot for that."

"What about a nice free massage? I wanna go to school for massage therapy anyway, so I can practice on you?"

"Thanks but no thanks. I'm good, I really gotta go."

"I'll give you a very happy ending, anything you want. I'll be your personal genie?"

"What? Young lady, are you soliciting sex?"

"No one has to know."

I instructed her to follow me, as I quickly got my keys and escorted her out into our hallway where security staff and other eye-witnesses were in clear view. "Look… give me a call Monday and I'll review your work and see what I can do…No promises, though!" As she exited the building, I couldn't help but feel sorry for her in that desperate state. She was willing to offer me sexual favors just so her EBT benefits wouldn't be cut off, as a result from being dropped.

The following Monday morning, she showed up bright and early with a professionally typed resume and additional job searches for her employer contact logs. I made one of the rarest exceptions and reversed her initial drop status to a completion. As she left the office with her certificate in hand, I realized that I did her a huge injustice by extending her job search assignments past the class enrollment deadline. I vowed from that moment on not to be an enabler to our addictive personality PTs. And from that day on, it's been no overtime continuation for them. They have three full weeks to submit all required documents otherwise risk benefits being affected. Far too often we become enablers to their welfare addiction. Addictive personalities come in various forms, and in a loving and healthier way, I had become addicted to Latte.

Holiday season 2007 was filled with mixed emotions as Latte called me up one night and shared some bad news. Ring, "Hey, sexy lady, how are you?"

"Ok, you?"

"It's the holidays and I'm in the holiday spirit, about to play some Donny Hathaway, 'This Christmas'…Oh…" as the silence suddenly gave way to a dark cloud over the phone.

"What's wrong, baby girl?"

"I have some bad news!"

"Uh Oh! What's going on?"

"I got a transfer from my job to North Carolina…"

"What? North Carolina? When?"

"I leave in a month."

"Wow, that's fast."

"Yeah, I'll be running a couple offices as district manager."

"Wow, congrats, sweetheart. That sounds like a wonderful career move for you?"

"It is. I'm excited about the career move, and the very affordable cost-of-living opportunities. However, I'm sad about leaving you… Come with me Babe, I hear that it's really affordable living and I know you can find a job out there…"

My heart sank, as my speech slurred to a slow-motion pace. "I can't leave my little-man…"

"I know. But I've fallen in love with you, and I want you and need you right by my side as I begin this new chapter in my life. I would also love for your son to come with us… We can be a family. Do you think his mom would consider relocating out there?"

After hanging up the phone with Latte, I turned off the living room lights to a pitch dark silence. This is one of my sanctuary moments where I reflect on life and my future. I turned on my stereo system as I was about to play one of my CDs when the Manhattans' "Shining Star" came on the radio. This was my favorite track from this group and I've heard it a million times before, but this time it was different, much different this time. The lyrics were singing specifically to Latte and me.

About an hour later, I call my son's mother just to pitch the relocation idea to her. Her response was that I can relocate, but our son stays here in California, court orders, remember? After a brief two-minute conversation with his mom, I knew the next phone call to Latte would be the goodbye call. I've cried over three women in my past…I mean balls-out break-down tears, and Latte was about to be one of them. After two and a half years of dating Latte, I realized that I sincerely loved that girl. I was so emotionally overwhelmed about the whole situation that the flood-gate of tears began to rush out of my eyes and I couldn't do a damn thing about it. It was one of my most heartfelt emotional break-down moments ever.

When it was all said and done, after my head was throbbing and I couldn't cry anymore, I knew I had to make that break-up call to Latte because, on July 20th, at 1:36pm, 1997, while standing over the mother of my child, I cut my son's umbilical cord, held him in my arms, and promised to never leave him. I loved Latte, but I love my Son much more. So with the saddest overtone, I called Latte back to decline the out-of-state relocation offer for the obvious aforementioned reason. It appeared that she got choked up because the conversation only lasted a few seconds more, and then she requested to meet up with me the following evening. After one of the longest sleepless nights of my life, we met up right after work that next day. The drive to her house felt like everything around me was in slow motion. Upon arriving at her house and thoroughly discussing all of our options, we agreed to see

YOU ME AND EBT

one another as often as possible over the next month until she left for North Carolina.

Thirty days came, and Latte was gone! Just like Michael Jackson's "She's Out of My Life" song… Latte was out of my life! Nonetheless, life goes on! And we both had to move on with our lives… Thank you for inspiring me to pursue my passion, Latte! I will never forget you.

CHAPTER 13: *The Audacity of His Story*

In our JSPC workshops, we're constantly motivating our PTs to never stop dreaming about achieving amazing careers, while oftentimes overcoming insurmountable odds! Encouraging them to set goals and passionately pursue those endeavors and all the while inspiring them to never giving up! There is one American story that truly epitomizes this premise.

It's January 3, 2008, I'm driving home from work, when I hear, Obama wins Iowa. I damn near hit the car in front of me as I pulled over, turned on KNX news radio, and that's all they were talking about…I couldn't believe Obama won the Iowa caucus? I thought, "It couldn't be!" With great interest, I raced home and tuned in to CNN, and watched my favorite political news source team both confirm and verify Obama's stunning caucus victory. Just like clock work, John King, one of CNN's political correspondents, checked a win next to Obama's name. I still couldn't believe it as I started listening to the other correspondents speak about this incredibly shocking opening primary/caucus season win for the Obama campaign. They spoke about how the small Iowa caucus was part of a 96% white population that didn't allow race/ethnicity to influence their vote. Obama beat out Senator John Edwards of North Carolina, and the golden girl, Senator Hillary Clinton of New York, who was favored to win the Democratic Party nomination. Well, things drastically changed that night because that win changed the whole entire political strategy for both the Edwards and Clinton camps, because no one saw Obama's Iowa caucus victory coming at all. Now Hillary did win the first New Hampshire primary nine days later; however, it was short lived because the Obama campaign put a strangle-hold lock on the entire primary/caucus season just a few weeks later.

On the evening of February 5, 2008, the Obama campaign put a shocking grip on the Democratic nomination process. No longer was he just the handsome young debonair Senator from Illinois who gave great inspirational speeches, this guy began to scare the living hell out of the Hillary camp and many super-delegates of the Democratic Party.

Many in the party, including myself, were shocked at the final Super Tuesday results. I remember standing up repeating: "No he didn't win, Colorado! No he didn't win, Alabama! What? He won Delaware? That's Joe Biden ground." As the CNN results continued displaying his victories in Connecticut, Idaho, Minnesota, North Dakota, Georgia, Illinois, Missouri, Utah, Alaska, Dorothy "ain't in Kansas anymore," I jumped up and down like I just read off my Big 6 California Lotto winning numbers. I couldn't believe this man won 13 of 24 Super-Tuesday states.

After watching an entire evening of CNN political pundits sift through what had happened, I knew I had to get involved with the Obama "Yes We Can" political movement. I made a $75 dollar pledge to his campaign and began seeking local Obama camps to get involved. The March, April, and May Primaries/Caucuses were just a mere formality because by the time the final Montana primary was tallied, Obama enjoyed a 1,763 pledged vote lead to Clinton's 1,640. And it didn't take long for Senator Hillary Clinton of New York to give one of the most historic concession speeches ever. Retraction! She gave the best political concession speech ever honoring those women in their 80s and 90s who didn't have the right to vote at the turn of the 20th century, those young girls/women who have been inspired by her campaign, those 18 million people who supported her. Now conceding the nomination by endorsing Senator Obama and embracing the campaign slogan, "Si Se Puede, Yes We Can."

Within a few days of that historic speech, 438 super-delegates tossed in their votes in order to push him over the 2,201 delegates needed to secure the party nomination. Many may ask, "Why is this story so significant?" Well, this is the story about a young man who overcame some incredible obstacles/challenges in his life to attain/achieve what many feel is the ultimate impossible American dream.

Barack Obama was born to a white mother from Kansas and an African foreign exchange student father from Kenya, in Honolulu, HI, back in 1961. His biological father divorced his mother and left the family when Obama was two years-old. Obama spent his early childhood years in Indonesia with Mom and Step-Dad, and his teenage years growing up in Honolulu with his maternal grandparents. He never stopped dreaming big about his future. Whether it was a brief enrollment at Occidental College in Los Angeles, CA, or undergraduate studies at Columbia University in NY, he never stopped dreaming about a bright future in America. Throughout his Harvard graduate years, community organizing days, and eight years as a junior senator and subsequent U.S Senator of Illinois, he never stopped dreaming! His eloquent 2004 Democratic keynote speech was a prelude of what he would become. Then on August 30, 2008, for the first time in American political history, Senator Barack Obama gave his nominee acceptance speech, and he accepted the Democratic nomination for President of the United States of America. After a week full of political heavy-weights like now deceased Senator Teddy Kennedy, and former Presidents Jimmy Carter and Bill Clinton, in front of over 75,000 people jam-packed in the Denver Colorado Convention Center, Senator Barack Obama gave another one of his polished presidential Democratic Nominee acceptance speeches. The two speeches I was totally keen on hearing were both Bill and Hillary Clinton's because I wasn't quite convinced that the bad blood between both camps was totally healed. There was a part of me that prepared for a party coup led by Bill, Hillary and their 256 super-delegate supporters.

However, when Hillary addressed the convention and spoke about how proud she was to be a mother, senator from New York, Democrat, an American, and supporter of Barack Obama, I pumped my clenched fist and said, "Yes, no coup! Hillary's fully on board now so I know Bill and the remaining 256 super-delegates will throw in their party support." With another eloquent speech, I couldn't help but admire Hillary even more. She is someone that you'd love to sit down with over a cup of coffee and have a long substantive political conversation. To me, no other former first lady could even hold a candle to her political knowledge, passion, and prowess that she brings to American politics. She blows the previous First Ladies out of the water. And Hillary's Harriet Tubman analogy about keep running, absolutely brilliant! Hillary's awesome! You go girl! Then her hubby Bill took the stage the very next night to a standing ovation crowd who couldn't help themselves but to say thanks for your global ambassador leadership, thanks for two exceptional presidential terms, thanks for 12 wonderful gubernatorial years as governor of Arkansas, thanks for your Harvard brilliance, thanks for your suave personality, thanks for displaying your musicianship as an accomplished saxophonist. Former President Bill Clinton gave a rousing speech, starting off by saying, "Hillary, myself, 18 million of you who supported her, now we must support Barack Obama as our next President of the United States." Per usual, Bill was insightful, eloquent, and presented a very good case on why we shouldn't support McCain. My favorite moment of the speech was when Bill said that 16 years ago they gave him the opportunity to run against the opposition who said that he was too young and lacked the political experience needed to be commander-in-chief. "Sound familiar?" he asked the crowd. Bill ended his speech by giving warm compliments about Barack being the 21st-century incarnation of the traditional American dream, and that his humanitarian strength and spirit will drive him as President to give all Americans–regardless of race, religion, sexual orientation, etc.–a fair shot at the American dream… Great job, Bill. You are, were, and will always be the greatest President of the 20th century.

President William Jefferson Clinton…

 True to form, Obama thanked the committee members who co-sponsored the event. And without even blinking an eye he accepted the party's nomination for Presidency of the United States with profound humility and gratitude. He acknowledged Bill and Hillary Clinton, acknowledged the love of his life Michelle, and the two daughters he loves dearly. As over 75,000 convention goers listened to every word uttered out of Obama's mouth with intent, sincerity, joy, jubilation, and emotional compassion, he reminded us of the story of a young woman from Kansas and a foreign exchange student from Kenya who got together at the University of Hawaii with a dream. He was a product of that dream and an example of how, through hard-work and determination, we all can fulfill our individual American dreams. Next he emphasized how this is a defining moment in our country's history, and how we cannot afford another four years of the same George W. Bush policies. My favorite moment of the speech was when Obama said to people across America, "Democrats, Republicans, Independents, enough! This moment and this election is our chance to keep the

American dream alive." He went on to say that on November 4th. We must say eight is enough.

As the general Presidential election campaign was getting under way, activities at my new worksite were soaring through the roof. The new site director empowered the activities committee to embrace the over 450 multi-culturally diverse staff to host fun-filled, educational, entertaining programs that would produce cohesiveness among staff and create an overall healthier work environment. When a couple of the activity leaders approached me about becoming involved in the programs, I enthusiastically agreed to offer my participatory services. However, little did I realize how much fun we were about to have over the next year. By the end of 2008, our site put on some amazing programs honoring Dr. Martin Luther King Jr., Cinco De Mayo, Mexican Independence, Asian Heritage, Armenian Cultural Traditions, and ended the year with a holiday district Christmas party that rocked the house.

On Tuesday, November 4th, 2008, our country made history. The dream came into fruition. Barack H. Obama became the first ever African-American President-elect. This is a powerfully motivating story that I share in all of my JSPC workshops. It's about never losing sight of your dreams, working hard towards achieving those dreams, and making a difference by embracing the endless opportunities to achieve success that our country has to offer. "Yes We Can" is so inspirational on so many levels! This Obama campaign slogan transcends ethnicity, age, gender, sexual orientation, faith, political affiliation, and economic status! It's a powerful reminder to us all, that we can pursue our passions, and achieve our dreams.

Unfortunately, the year didn't quite end on the most up-beat note regarding the worsening conditions of our PTs; however, our staff and fellow colleagues were truly unifying. Allow me to share some of the unfortunate behavioral incidents that took place at the new site.

We had several county police take-downs of unruly PTs, increases in domestic violence lobby incidences, mental health barriers, substance abuse challenges. One day, one of my mental health staff colleagues passed by one of our job search rooms and witnessed a female PT in a wheelchair perform oral copulation on one of our male PTs. When my colleague started yelling at them to stop, the girl sucked harder until he successfully ejaculated into her mouth… Wow! What a sticky situation that was, huh?

On another occasion, I was coming down from the second floor side stairway when I observed a female PT finger-penetrating another female PT against the side wall. When I verbally confronted the two young ladies–from a safe distance, about their inappropriate public display of affection, the one doing the finger-penetrating responded by saying, "Hold on, we'll be finished in a minute." Well, what was I supposed to do, break them up? I just calmly walked over and alerted one of our security staff to handle the situation. However, when the security staff went over to the scene of the finger-banging crime, both young ladies fled the scene. I guess the young lady was correct when she said they'd be finished in a minute…

Things were getting so bad that our mental health staff was getting cursed out and threatened on a regular basis! I was coming from lunch one day when all I could hear was, "Bitch! I will cut you!" I immediately kept walking around the cubicle area where a PT was in a striking motion towards one of our mental health staff just seconds before security and county police officers descended on the scene to apprehend and arrest the attacker. As I headed back to my desk area, I realized that this job had become much more dangerous than ever before. So to relieve the mounting stress of PT threats, oversized enrollment classes and overloaded caseloads, many of my colleagues began to really embrace our site program functions. That was our time to let our hair down, unwind a bit, sing, dance, perform, and really enjoy the program entertainment. Inevitably, these site challenges allowed us to grow even stronger as a professional family however; nothing could have prepared me for the personal family loss I was about to experience.

CHAPTER 14: *Forever Family*

By the time holiday season 2008 came around, while many of us Americans were still celebrating the historic presidential landslide victory a few weeks earlier, I received one of the saddest family news of my life thus far-that my maternal grandmother Lillian Lee was diagnosed with inoperable colon cancer. I received the news earlier in the week from my mom via phone as she flew back east to be by her dying mother's side. Within a week of my mother's arrival, my Nana, Lillian Lee, died holding my mom's hand as her spirit departed from her flesh, ascending to be with her Lord and Savior Jesus Christ! After 89 years on this earth, Lillian's mission was complete, and our Eternal Commander-In-Chief summoned her to join the other countless spirits in everlasting life... Talk about highs/lows all within a short period of time. I knew I had to fly back east to be with my mom and the rest of my east coast family. We all shared so many Lillian stories that I could feel her spirit sitting down with all of us laughing away. Lillian Lee entered this earth back in 1919, to West Indian and African-American parents. She was an avid churchgoer, where she played the piano for her church choir. She dropped out of school as a young teenager and married my maternal grandfather, Weaver Lee. Granddaddy Lee served our country with bravery/dignity in our military service. They raised six children–four girls and two boys. These were my two uncles, three aunts, and one extraordinary woman I call mom! I have the absolute best Mom on earth! She's the number one lady in my life! Love you, Mommy!!!

The funniest thing about my grandparents is they were total opposites. My granddad worked hard during the day for the state of Connecticut and partied hard all night with his drinking buddies. Much love for Granddaddy Lee who took care of our Nana for over 40 years before succumbing to a heart attack back in 1982. And when he passed away, the house was paid off, with enough savings to cover property taxes for years to come and additional savings/investments that lasted our Nana another 20 years before we all had to start financially help off-set certain monthly costs. It was the summer of 1975, and my mother was going through what I now know was an extremely difficult divorce, so she sent us 3,000 miles away to spend the summer with Nana and Granddaddy Lee while she planned the next move for my sister and me. As my Auntie Barbara brought us over to our grandparents' huge three story home that sat on 1.5 acres of land, I said, *Wow! Their house is bigger than ours!* We exited the car like two kids racing into Disneyland. Our Nana was the first to greet my Auntie Nita, my sister Ingrid, and myself. I remember her giving us the biggest bear-hug I ever received. Without even the opportunity to unpack our suitcases, upon entering the house Granddaddy Lee had us sit down at the kitchen table while he laid down strict house rules. I remember staring at my sister while this gray-haired man rambled on and on and on about every detail of the house rules, when, saved by the bell, our Nana rescued us by saying, "Look Weaver Lee, our grandkids came all the way from California, they'll have all summer long to get used to your military house rules, let them relax. You kids hungry?"

"Yes Nana!"

She whipped us up a sandwich just to tie us down until her world-class chef dinner later that evening. After a wonderful nine-course chicken dinner meal complete with baked potato, veggies, homemade cornbread, iced tea, we capped off the night with some sweet potato pie, and an 8:30 bedtime.

The next day is when my sister and I made our round-robin family tour of duty introductions. By the end of the day, we met 13 of our cousins and our other two aunts. That first weekend was very fun as we went swimming, bowling, and attended a family backyard barbecue. By weekend's end, I was spent! I was thinking that I'd be able to sleep in a bit that following Monday morning, but Granddaddy had another idea in mind. It's early Monday morning, and I was awakened to my Granddaddy's voice, "Rise and shine, Sport. Wash up and eat some cereal, you're gonna hang-out with your Granddaddy today."

"Yes sir!" I washed up, ate a quick bowl of cereal, and rolled out with my grandfather. Little did I know he would take me to his job and serve as my neighborhood tourist guide through some of the less desirable sections of East Hartford, CT. We then drove to his place of employment and pulled into the parking lot of his job, where he worked in the Social Services Department for the State of Connecticut. The only thing I remember is him proudly parading me around the office and introducing me as his grandson from California to a lot of friendly white people dressed nicely. Upon leaving his worksite, we began driving down the less desirable neighborhoods where he pointed out various winos, bums, drug addicts, and working day girls. It was a teachable moment for me because he began to explain how people make choices in life to have a good life or a bad life. I remember asking him, "Why doesn't the government help them have a better life?"

"I work for that government you're talking about, and we do help them. However, too often, they don't help themselves."

"What do you mean by that, Granddaddy?"

"You see, son, most of these people chose to drop out of school, get hooked on drugs, and they became family outcasts, and then they expected society to take care of them."

"What kind of help do you give them?"

"They get food, shelter, substance-abuse treatment, mental health services, job training, and educational assistance from us."

"Then why are they still living on the streets?"

"It's a choice they made, son. The government can provide all the services in the world to help these people. However, if they don't want to help themselves then it's all for naught." I'll never forget that conversation with my Granddaddy, because what he said over 36 years ago remains true today in social services. Both the state and federal governments can offer every social services assistance program known to mankind, but if the recipients don't want to help themselves, then it's all for naught! Those were prophetically powerful words spoken by my Granddaddy, the social services prophet, back in 1975. Until this day, there's not a workshop I facilitate, nor does a class go by, where I don't think about his powerful prophetic words. Thanks Granddaddy, your social services spirit lives on vicariously through me... love you! The rest of that summer was fun-filled with a whole lot of family activities capped off by the celebration of my mom's birthday. As we all sang happy birthday to her, it was almost like she was physically there but not emotionally with us. Now, of course I was way too young to understand adult separations/divorces; however, that was the reality of what our family of four was going through at the time. At the conclusion of my mom's birthday celebration, we said our good-byes to everyone, got to bed at the normal 8:30pm hour, and prepared to catch the TWA flight back to Los Angeles the next day. The next morning as we were packing the remaining souvenirs from Nana, Granddaddy took me outside to the front patio and told me to listen to my mother and be strong for her. I understood the listen to my mother part, but the part about being strong for her really didn't sink in until we got back to California. He gave me a big hug and wanted me to know that he loved me and my sister, and that we'll always have a family in Hartford, CT who loves us very much, and their doors would always be open to us. After that porch moment with Granddaddy, we both re-entered the house and finalized the remaining packing duties. And within a few short hours, we headed to the airport, embraced in final goodbye hugs, and boarded the TWA flight headed for LAX. Five hours later, we landed into LAX airport and were received by my Auntie Nita. The ride back home was filled with conversations about our summer trip back home to Hartford and a dinner stop-over at Carrows restaurant in Gardena.

We got home to an empty house, hit the showers, and went to bed. The next day Moms informed us that she and our father were divorcing and that he would come pick us up every other weekend. The news was shocking to me because I had no clue of what was going on. Growing up in Hartford, CT during the 1960s, my parents were high school sweethearts. My dad was my mom's first true love. She loved that man with all of her heart, unfortunately, Dad was diagnosed with severe manic depression, which would be today's version of severe bipolar disorder. Back in the early 1970s, society categorized his condition as mentally ill, insane, or crazy. When my mom explained his condition as a chemically-imbalanced blood disorder, I couldn't comprehend what she was saying until I started visually witnessing his illness firsthand.

You see, my dad entered the U.S. Army right out of high school, and began a welter-weight boxing career that garnered him many headlines in the boxing world as an up-and-coming world-class welter-weight prize fighter. With my sister in my mom's womb, they relocated to one of the Louisiana army bases, where they adjusted to the military base family lifestyle. Somewhere between the years of 1967 and 1972, with an 18-4 professional boxing record with nine knockouts, my father's condition had worsened. His boxing career was over and had literally torn apart a marriage. Several UCLA medical studies concluded a chemical imbalance in the blood triggered his manic depression illness, coupled with early signs of Parkinson's disease. What a mouthful for my dad to deal with and a handful for my mom to cope with... I remember a lot of fun early years going to the downtown L.A. boxing gym watching and training with my dad and other boxers. I would follow along his jump-roping, speed bag, heavy bag, and light sparring ring sessions regimen. He introduced me to martial arts at an early age; my sister and I participated in many of his side passion theatrical plays at L.A.'s downtown inner-city theatre. It was all confusing to me. Physically he looked fine. Nevertheless, he needed to take medication in order to suppress his violent outbursts...

For the next couple of months during the fall of 1975, our dad would pick us up like clockwork every other weekend, until early spring of 1976, when things permanently changed. It was early spring 1976, and my sister and I were at our neighborhood babysitter's house on the southwest side of the city of Gardena, CA. Our babysitter summoned me over to the kitchen window to witness something that has stayed with me to this very day. For the first time ever, I had an eye-witness account of one of his outwardly displayed manic depression performances in our back-yard. It shook me up pretty bad! My mouth dropped as I stared for what seemed like an eternity... He was obviously off his medication and acting out what his professional medical evaluators called "episodes." Still shocked at what I had witnessed, not a few weeks later, my dad entered my bedroom like nothing ever happened and said, "Hey son, whatcha doing?"

"Playing with my G.I. Joe," I responded.

"Your mom and I are back together again, isn't that great news?"

"Yeah, dad."

Soon as my dad went to lie down to take a nap, my mom quickly rushed my sister and me out of the house. With nothing more than my boxing shoes, a tough-skins outfit, and my G.I. Joe action figure, mom packed two suitcases, our Auntie Nita picked us up, and we never returned to our beautiful English castle home again. I remember sitting in the back seat of my Aunties car, feeling powerless. I knew my father was mentally ill, but I couldn't do anything to help him. All I wanted to do was go back home and wake up from that bad dream. However, I had to quickly snap out of hoping it was a bad dream and face the reality. Nevertheless, I knew I had to be the strongest eight year-old at that moment for my mother. Not much conversation took place as I sat in the back seat reflecting on all the good times and fun memories we had in our castle-home. You see, our block was literally the United Nations of families. We had Cuban, Filipino, Japanese, Hawaiian, White, Mexican, Jewish, Chinese, Black, and Italian families. The surrounding neighborhood comprised Korean, Samoan, and various other Hispanic cultures. All of us neighborhood kids played every indoor/outdoor game imaginable.

It was truly a great community. Sadness came over me, not knowing if I'd ever play with or see my friends again. I had to muster up all the strength inside of me not to cry and remain supportive and strong for both my sister and my mom. Here I was, just an eight year-old kid and already assuming the man of the household role, or so I thought. After a few months of staying with various family members, we finally settled in on the east-side of Gardena, in a section affectionately called "the alley." Yes, we down-sized from a beautiful English castle home on the safe southwest side of Gardena to the worst run-down section on the east side of Gardena. After three months of living with family members, "the alley" was our new home. Little did I know that my mom's new male friend would be moving in with us.

When my parents first came to Gardena back in 1971, they were introduced to Nichiren Soshu of America (NSA), now renamed Soka Gakkai International or SGI. In 1960, President Daisoku Ikeda, brought to the United States, the ancient Japanese teachings of a monk name Nichiren. Nichiren introduced the Sanskrit (devote oneself) teachings of the Lotus Sutra to Japanese followers around 1253 A.D. The basic principles of the Sutra are: The universe is one whole single living entity; individuals must practice these teachings through devotion in order to gain-strength, wisdom, happiness, enlightenment, and empowerment. Devotion was accomplished in several major ways: chanting, Nam, (devote oneself), Myoho (mystic law that says truth governs mystic law of the universe), Renge (lotus flower), and Kyo (sutra voice-teaching of Buddha). Between chanting Shakabuku (witnessing to non practicing SGI members), today over 12 million members continue this global cause for universal peace and oneness.

After my parents split up and subsequently divorced, one of the SGI members introduced my mom to her son. They evidently were secretly dating for awhile because next thing I know, this guy was moving in with us into what we affectionately called "the alley." The only thing the lady forgot to tell my mother, my sister and me was the previous lifestyle her son led. The man who would eventually become my stepfather served time in one of Hawaii's juvenile camps, came to southern California in the late 1960s, started pimping by the early 1970s, in/out of jail. His best friend was a member of the Japanese mafia family, Yakuza, and one of his other childhood hang-out buddies was on America's Most Wanted list for murder. Needless to say, my new stepfather and his unique set of friends gave me a whole new perspective of fantasy vs. reality. Fantasy was on television and at the movie theaters; we lived a different reality for years to come…

Why is sharing this part of my life's story so relevant to this book? Because oftentimes our PTs pre-judge us facilitators and think that we can't relate to their current conditions and struggles! On the contrary! Many of my colleagues, including myself, have gone through similar and or even worse challenges than our PTs face. Nevertheless, we've made conscious decisions to progressively move forward in our lives… So now its holiday season 2008, and my fellow colleagues are ready to get their boogie, groove, funk, hip-hop, rock, party on! We entered the venue to see my female colleagues dressed like they were presenters of the Golden Globes award show. The fellas had a mixture of business casual, corporate conservative, to club "pimping ain't easy" dress attire. A few of us hit the sports bar for a few happy hour drinks while watching the holiday party guests trickle in. The remainder of the evening was like Vegas: what went on there stayed there! In addition to having a wonderful event, I pitched an idea to our director about having an award show that recognizes the hard work and contributions of our front-line staff each fiscal year. The awards show idea was directly inspired by Steve Harvey's "Hoodie Awards." However, we would call our award show the "Swoodie Awards." Steve Harvey is one of America's iconic, legendary comedians who introduced the first annual Hoodie Awards back in 2000. The basic concept of Steve Harvey's award show was to recognize, acknowledge, and award small businesses in the community who may not otherwise have gotten recognized for their business contributions to communities all throughout our country. The award categories consisted of Best Church, Beauty Salon, Restaurant, Barber Shop, Car Wash, Community Leader, etc. Therefore, my idea was for our district to have "best" categories such as Custodial Crew, Security/County Police, Eligibility Worker/Case Manager, Supervisor/Management, Fundraiser/Activity Member, Special Recognitions, etc. Our district director gave us her blessings along with the green light to make it happen.

CHAPTER 15: *Bring On 2009*

As the New Year 2009 arrived, I had no idea how busy we would be with over-enrollment in classes and increased PT drama while developing a new awards show. We began 2009 with a wonderful Black History Month celebration, and I had the distinct honor of reciting a piece of the Rev. Dr. Martin Luther King Jr.'s 1963 historic "I Have a Dream" speech! The program theme was "From Slavery to the Historic March on Washington." The atmosphere in the room in front of over 300 of our fellow colleagues was electric. My portion came at the very end of the program where I had prepared to recite the final three minutes of that speech, leading up to the finale, "Free At Last! Free At Last!" When I approached the podium, it felt like the living spirit of Dr. King entered my body and spoke through my mouth. It was one of the most incredible public speaking moments I've ever experienced! As I got to the "let freedom ring" portion of the condensed speech, you could hear a pin drop in the room. At that moment, it wasn't me speaking–it was the amazing spirit of one of the greatest martyrs of human rights in the 20th century, the Rev. Dr. Martin Luther King Jr., and when the spirit of Dr. King got to "Free at last! Free at last! Thank God Almighty, we are free at last!" his spirit left my body, and I sat down in awe of what had just happened. Now, upon completion of the speech, I informed my colleagues that Dr. King's spirit was present here today. It was like the spirit of Dr. King reminding us all that we are now free–free to have the most fulfilling, abundant life because our ancestors paved the way and paid the price through protest against social inequalities, injustices, government policies, and bloodshed.

As I went back into my office and sat back down at my desk, I decided to sincerely remind our PTs that there are so many employment/career opportunities out there; we just have to be flexible and open to opportunities as they present themselves. It's about EMPOWERMENT! No more spoon-feeding, burping, changing diapers of able-bodied grown folks. I would now fully embrace the scripture, "give a man a fish, he'll eat for a day–teach him how to fish, he'll eat for life." The epiphany was the realization that we were doing our PTs a huge disservice by super-duper babying them as opposed to empowering them to make a positive change for their future. Here are the implementations I've made moving forward as a facilitator. I reminded the very next class I facilitated that if you don't have a high school diploma/GED, it's time to get the ball rolling and enroll in somebody's GED program. If you have mental health challenges, seek mental health services. If you can't pass the drug test, enroll in a substance abuse treatment program. If you have a felony and/or felonies on your record, seek our felony expungement workshop classes or seek other legal means to earn a living. It is now our time to be held accountable, responsible, and amenable to progressive change for the betterment of a positive future. No more pacifying swipes of EBT cards, it's now about empowering us to set goals today, so we can have a fighting chance to experience the amazing possibilities of a bigger, better, brighter future of tomorrow.

I told one of my JSPC workshop classes that our President is a living example of the incredible opportunities the United States of America has to offer. "It's our choice, people! "We can choose to push a shopping cart down Figueroa Street by day and sleep on a park bench by night, or we can own the grocery store; we can cry about not having diplomas/degrees or we can identify a school and career choice and qualify for state/federal grants/loans to pay for cost of tuition, books, room/board, etc. We can complain about age discrimination as a barrier or use it as an advantage for those employers seeking mature, dependable employees. We can allow racism to prevent us from a successful career or walk through the major door our President just opened. We can argue that many employers won't hire certain or all felons, or we can do like our three amigos from San Diego who creatively started their own small business moving company. It is no longer acceptable to make passive excuses for our problems. Let's take aggressive action towards progressive solutions. There are way too many past, present, and future success stories out there for us to wallow in "poor ole me!" Pity parties are played out! It's now time for all of us to be held accountable for our own successes and failures. Now it's time for all of us to be responsible for setting present-day goals; now it's time to pay forward an attainable, rewarding future." The class looked at me like I had smoked some crack! Then the feedback came rushing out. I was called insensitive, unrealistic, non-compassionate, even an elitist–go figure! I always allow my classes to totally express themselves verbally as long as they're not threatening bodily harm, using inappropriate/ aggressive profanity, or being blatantly disrespectful to their fellow classmates or me.

Next on the agenda, our Mexican and Hispanic colleagues put on an amazing Cinco De Mayo observance celebration. They did a wonderful job differentiating between the battle of Puebla and the actual Mexican Independence. On the 5th of May, 1862, the non-favored Mexican Army's military victory over the French was celebrated in the state of Puebla and now recognized and observed in the United States; however, many Mexicans in the U.S. and Mexico embrace Mexican Independence Day as their true victory for Mexico's independence. It was the 16th of September, 1810, when a Mexican coalition army led by Father Miguel Hidalgo (priest, well educated, dean of college, courageous humanitarian), and Ignacio Allende (Spanish-born into the wealthy Criollos family, served as captain of Spanish army, compassionate towards a new Spain and the Mexican Independence movement), gathered Queretaro (state official), Corridor of Queretaro (lead state official), his wife, mestizos and Indians. They marched through battlesfields dominating their enemies with clubs, slings, axes, knives, and machetes on their way to Mexico City where they claimed independence victory over the Spanish by confiscating the picture of Guadalupe. After over 300 years of Spanish and French control, the Mexican natives of Mexico finally had true sovereign country independence… Viva Mexico!

I often share with our JSPC classes about how we can bring the fun to most work environments, just as this site has done. By Memorial Day of 2009, our Swoodie committee had developed the Swoodie award categories: Best Security/County Police, Best Chef, Best Custodial Staff, Best Supervisor, Best Admin/Clerical Staff, Best Fundraiser, Best Sense of Humor, Best Personality, Best Entertainer, Special Senior Staff Award, Special Postpartum Award, and Special Director's Award.

We scheduled our Swoodie Best Chef kick-off event on the 16th of July,
and planned on three categories per month voting leading up to the
finale Holiday Party/Swoodie Awards December 18, 2009.

Now, by the end of June 2009, it was time for a little R&R, so I flew out
to New Mexico to spend a week with the #1 lady in my life, my mama!
My Southwest Airlines flight–where bags fly free!–arrived at Albuquerque's only airport. I de-boarded the cabin corridor and began to
appreciate the calmness of the airport's ambiance, the politeness of
airport passengers, and golden lullaby sounds of baggage claim dis-
pensing my luggage. The serendipitous sounds of the night's warm air
massaged my face as I awaited the arrival of my mother to pick me up.
Within 10 minutes, Moms swooped me up in her smooth luxury edi-
tion 2008 Chevy Malibu. We gave each other a warm mama bear and
baby cub hug, I loaded the roll-away luggage into the trunk, and we
headed to her house. My mom has a beautiful four-bedroom, three-
bath 2200–square-foot bi-level home, with a gorgeous gazebo overlooking the huge backyard. Visiting Mom is my oasis away from the
hustle and bustle of Los Angeles. It's where I love to go and regroup
my thoughts and plans for a progressive future. Everyone who's familiar with L.A. knows that after most LAX experiences you need a shot
of rum or vodka. Just safely getting to curbside parking for depart-
ing flights is a dangerous adventure. Between buses trying to run you
over, taxicabs performing dangerous stunt driving tactical maneuvers,
police ready to cite you, and just flat-out impatient/rude travelers and
their loved ones, LAX is definitely not one of my favorite hang-out
places in the world.

Each day in New Mexico, I awakened to the harmonious sounds of
my mom's backyard birds, breakfast conversations with Moms, and
spontaneous unplanned activities for the day. The many small business arts, crafts, and museums pay homage to the authentic heritage
of both Indian and Hispanic cultures. This was a nice trip to unwind/
relax, and spend some quality time with my mom, just a few months
removed of the passing of our nana. And, then unexpectedly on June
25, 2009, Michael Joseph Jackson was rushed to Cedar Sinai Medical
Center in Los Angeles, CA, at approximately 12:20pm. Around 3:45pm,

Albuquerque time, one of my uncles called my mom to share the tragic news that Michael Joseph Jackson was pronounced dead at 2:26 pm PST. Upon receiving that news, all I wanted to do was rush back to my mom's house and absorb myself in the news details. For me, it all started back in the summer of 1973, when little 14 year-old Michael sang "Ben" in front of a live Oscars audience in L.A. I became a fan at that moment. Whether he and/or his brothers were singing "I Want You Back," "Rockin-Robin," "I'll be There," "ABC," "She's Outta My Life," "Blame It On The Boogie," "Dancing Machine," "Off The Wall," "Don't Stop 'Til You Get Enough," "Rock With You," "Working Day and Night," "Heartbreak Hotel," "Wanna Be Startin' Something," "The Girl Is Mine," "Beat It," "Billie Jean," "Thriller," "PYT," "Human Nature," "The Way You Make Me Feel," "I'm Bad," "Man In The Mirror," "Smooth Criminal," "Butterflies," or "Heal The World," Michael Joseph Jackson was and always will be the world's greatest entertainer. Rest In Peace, King of PoP.

Upon my return home to California, I was inspired to include a Michael Jackson tribute of some sort. So when I pitched the idea to a few of my colleagues and district site director, everyone was fully on board with total support. Now the only problem was getting enough talented people together to pull off a mini-concert musical tribute to Michael in the short time given. In between preparing for our July Cook-off/ Swoodie Kick-off, facilitating orientation classes, teaching JSPC classes, and Swoodie meetings, we had to round up staff to begin rehearsals for our August 27th "Michael Jackson Day Remembered" program. Chef entry requests came within a few days after announcing the cook-off category. It's July 16, 2009, and we had 12 samples of ethnic dishes ranging from Asian, soul food, Mexican, Armenian, Italian, including vegetables and desserts. Over 375 of our colleagues participated in this Swoodie Cook-off/Kick-off fundraiser, and our Swoodie staff received warm compliments on how well the event turned out. Each chef also received congratulatory praises for their tasty and quality edible samples. Upon the completion/clean-up of our very successful Swoodie Kick-off, those of us who were part of the Michael Jackson birthday remembrance recognition knew we had our work cut out for us with a month and a half to prepare. Until the end of July, our Michael Jackson Committee worked our tails off providing quality services to our PTs during the day while rehearsing all aspects of the program–after work hours were over–in our staff lounge. Now, there was just one problem: We didn't have all the talent for the program, nor did we have the program format detailed until two weeks before we were slated to perform…yes! It was stress time! During this period, we all put in long work hours, rehearsal hours and additional practice hours at home. The lady in charge of leading 18 of us in the "Thriller" dance portion was absolutely amazing! This girl needs to be doing professional choreography—she was that good. Capricorn and Lady E were working on a lovely "She's Outta My Life" duet. Our colleague Al was preparing a brilliant poem, some of the fellas and I were working on a couple of Jackson 5 hits like "I Want You Back" and "Man In The Mirror." And our site engineer was preparing our world-class sound studio.

The program was coming together with incredible speed, cohesiveness, and unity. With three Swoodie categories already in the ballot boxes, it was time to show our appreciation for Michael. With the excitement buzzing in our building's air and anticipation brewing amongst our anxious performers, I have to admit that I was incredibly pumped to hit that stage in honor of Michael. I could barely sleep the night before, and I had to control my enthusiasm the day of the performance because I knew we were about to blow the audience away with an incredible tribute. Thursday morning August 27, 2009, was a warm summer day. I had just finished facilitating the morning orientation class and it was lunchtime. I knew I couldn't eat heavy because show time started at 2:30, and we had to go over a final dress rehearsal walkthrough of the performance order at 1:30pm. So I decided to keep it light: a vegetable roll and inari(Japanese tofu sushi) from my favorite Sushi Boy restaurant in Gardena. That was a perfect decision because after that meal I felt like Popeye had just eaten his spinach! I felt energized! I headed back to the building by 1pm, shut my office door in silence/privacy, and said a grateful prayer. Then I headed upstairs to meet my fellow co-performing colleagues. As I entered our master conference room, I felt the incredible energy, spirit, power and essence of what Michael meant to so many of us growing up. At approximately 2:20pm, one of our well-respected colleagues led us in a very meaningful prayer, then we all preceded down to the main performing lounge where over 400 of our co-workers were jam-packed awaiting the start of the program. Our boy Low-Key got the party started with his various magical PowerPoint clips of old Michael Jackson perform-ance footage, while I entered the room to emcee/greet everyone to our Michael Joseph Jackson Birthday/Remembrance Celebration.

Big Al kicked things off by reciting a most heartfelt/memorable poem about Michael. We followed up with a brief "I Want You Back" per-formance. A few more PowerPoint video clips of Michael during the "Off The Wall" era, and clips of the Motown 25 live show. Next, my boy Capricorn, and my girl Lady E, hit the audience with a tear-jerking extremely emotional, "She's Out of My Life" duet rendition, followed by an audience participation of "Man In The Mirror"! We then took a brief ice cream sundae intermission while we prepared ourselves with monster "Thriller" make-up in the dressing room.

During this time we kept the audience involved with another staff per-formance solo, and a couple more clips. As our resident make-up artist caked 18 of us up with that "Thriller"-video-look make-up, the audi-ence was anxiously awaiting the finale… We all entered the dark audi-torium-size staff room with "Thriller" playing and voices of cheer from our colleagues. We proceeded to flat out rip the "Thriller" dance moves to where the audience gave us a standing ovation. It was an adrena-line rush to say the least! At the conclusion of the performance and program, we were all grateful to receive gracious congratulations from our fellow colleagues for such a magnificent performance/program. Now I know what some people are thinking, *Why Michael? Wasn't his life marred and scarred by his bizarre behavior? Vitiligo, Captain Crunch Outfits, Elephant Man bones, Wacko Jacko, Peter Pan, oxygen tanks, mask, over-the-balcony infant hanging, alleged child molestation allegations?* I can honestly say that as a father myself, I always prayed that the child molestation allegations weren't true. And as a human being, I'm not qualified to judge his likes/dislikes, nor imperfections; all I know is that he had a unique God-given talent that he shared with the world. He was put on this earth to ENTERTAIN us! That was his life's calling and mission! Who am I to judge someone deciding to dress the way he did, or have certain surgical plastic procedures done to his body, or collect very eccentric items. Now, dangling little man over the balcony was a bit over-the-top, but I think he was caught in the moment of complete fatherly joy. The point is, I'm not in a position of perfection to judge anyone, nor is any other human being qualified to cast judgment on another fellow imperfect human being. Nonetheless, the entertainment legacy that Michael left us was an extraordinary one! I encourage all of our PTs to embrace their God-given talents, set goals, pursue their passions, and work toward achieving those goals each and every day. Thanks for reminding us of that Michael!

In September of that same year, we showcased a "Puttin' on the Hits" program, where several acts performed for our Entertainer of the Year Swoodie category. By this time, our Swoodie voting was off the charts. Enthusiastic momentum was in full force! The acts were incredible. That site/district has some of the most–correction!—THE most talented DPSS staff in the entire county of Los Angeles, CA. From poetry-gospel, to singing and dancing, they're second to none. I had the idea for a few of us fellas to get a pretend band together and lip-sync to a choreographed performance of an old funk group. Instantly, I thought of my favorite 80s funk band, The Time, featuring Morris Day. Ok, now, I had to round up Jerome, Jimmy Jam, Terry Lewis, and at least Jesse Johnson. When I first pitched the idea to Capricorn, he jumped on board instantly by calling first dibs on Jerome. I said, "Cool!" (No Morris Day pun intended!) I got my Jerome, now I just need to get the other fellas. The Time casting call took about a week, then we only had two weeks to prepare for our performance.

By the end of that casting-call week, I had successfully recruited The Time band members. Mr. Low-Key was Jesse Johnson, Smooth L. was Jimmy Jam, Notre Dame was Terry Lewis, Capricorn was Jerome, and I was Morris Day. What pressure we put on ourselves, right? Yep! We sure as hell did. Next, we had to come up with a song that would rock da house, set it off, tear the roof off the mutha. The song that immediately came to mind after finalizing the line-up for our act was "The Bird! Come on now America, have you heard? That brand new dance it's called The Bird! Don't need no finesse or no personality..." That song is dang near The Time's national anthem! What an incredibly written, arranged and performed party song by Morris Day and

The Time. Besides, I was a big Morris Day fan back in the day. So, once again, in between facilitating orientation motivation sessions, teaching JSPC classes, one-on-one sessions, staff meetings, Swoodie meetings, ballot voting duties, and now Morris Day and The Time rehearsals, fatigue turned into adrenaline. We rehearsed daily for a week straight after work. Each rehearsal was met with increased excitement and confidence. It was tiring but fun. At the end of each night I made sure I took long baths and got plenty of rest, so that I would be re-energized for the next day. Meanwhile, the buzz around the Swoodie Awards voting and the scheduled upcoming holiday party really got people involved in the voting process, fundraisers, participation in all site events. We were generating very nice fundraising proceeds up until Thanksgiving time.

It was time, no pun intended! On September 17th 2009, our "Puttin' on the Hits" showcase was under way. The acts were incredible! The poetry reading, rap singing, gospel skit, Ike & Tina performance, a couple of live solo acts, then we were the last act to perform. When the opening music of "The Bird" came on, we hit the stage like we were really Morris Day and The Time…and when many in the audience began to stand up doing the Bird dance with the group, it almost felt like doing the wave at a sporting event. The audience participation was awesome! That gave us all motivation to hype our performance up even more to where almost everybody in the audience was on their feet dancing and grooving right along with us, doing The Bird. I really do understand what performers and entertainers mean when they describe the feeling they get when they're performing on stage. When you see those smiling faces singing or dancing along with you, you feel their energy flowing towards the stage. It's like a highly contagious energy flu floating in the air, and we're all contaminated/infected. It's an absolutely incredible natural high that no drug can match!

At the conclusion of "Puttin' on the Hits" program, everyone approached us with overwhelming flattering remarks/comments. We were all really appreciative of such a warm response! Our site director even asked us to do a special encore performance at our 2009 holiday district party. On behalf of the group, we accepted. That was the moment I realized that I was addicted to performing. It's like a drug to me! I just can't get enough! I want more! I need more! It's an insatiable appetite that I love to satisfy. For the months leading up to our December 18th holiday party, our class sizes really began to increase in numbers. The economic recession had taken its toll on all industries and unemployed job seekers, which made our jobs increasingly more challenging/difficult. Nevertheless, all of our site programs became therapy for many of us because it gave way to another form of healthy release. It's the 18th of December, 2009, and I arrived at our holiday party function around 6:30 pm to help set up and assist with our red-carpet interviews as guests began arriving around 7:15 pm. The ladies were wearing evening dresses/outfits that could have rivaled any Oscar red-carpet wardrobes. They looked absolutely stunning! The men showed up representing in suits, and a few of us fellas were sporting tuxedos! It was the finest red-carpet preview to a holiday party the District has ever seen.

Dinner was served at approximately 8:00 pm, and annual introductions, recognitions, and door prizes were given. At approximately 8:45pm, it was time to begin the Swoodie portion of the holiday party. A couple of us tuxedo fellas approached the stage with the "Mission Impossible" theme song playing in the background and announced the hidden ballot votes/winners of each Swoodie category. We gave it that Price-Waterhouse flavor introduction/explanation. The first act was us carrying Lady E onto the stage as she sat on a makeshift snow sled singing "Santa Baby" dressed up in a red/white sexy Santa outfit Christmas suit. Many men in the audience gasped throughout her performance. She was sexy and seductive with a whole lot of tasteful appropriateness all wrapped up in one. Lady E was simply gorgeous!

As the other wonderful acts hit the stage to do their thing, the fellas and I had to hit the dressing room and change clothes for our Morris Day and The Time performance. When it was time for our performance, we entered through the exit doors, ran on stage and began our opening dance routine to "The Bird." The audience instantly stood up and began mimicking the Bird dance. It was so much fun! And many awards were given out that night. Everything from Best Custodial-

Supervisor to Best Clerical Staff-Fundraiser. The final award was given to me for Best Entertainer! I was moved, appreciative, and grateful that my colleagues supported/voted for me. I thanked them from the bottom of my heart and hoped that we could continue having meaningful programs like this in the future.

CHAPTER 16: *Let's Play Job Search*

January of 2010 began with me needing a break. I took some well-deserved vacation time off just to rest, relax, sleep, and just simply chill/recuperate from a non-stop 2009. It also marked the beginning of a new era in holding our PTs truly accountable for their GAPS job search efforts. Yes, our economy was and still is recovering from the second worst economic disaster in our nation's history. However, way too many of our PTs were falsifying job searches to a ridiculous level. Each site would assist them with job development, PTs have Internet access for online application purposes as well as community work-source centers, family/friends, and additional community resources at their disposal. What was a significant portion of PTs doing, however? They were falsifying job searches. During the two-week job search portion of their average three-week JSPC classes, our PTs are required to conduct anywhere from three to five job searches daily with employers that are hiring. The idea of such demanding daily searches is the old adage that job search is a numbers game. The more applications and resumes a job seeker has out there in the job market, the chances of getting call-backs and interviews greatly increase. The fewer applications out there, the chances for call-backs/interviews diminish. Sounds logical, right? The more we put into something, the more we'll get out of it, right?

Let me ask all you hard-working taxpayers a question. If you knew that anywhere between $400-$600 a month of your hard-working state/federal taxes are going to a person who is definitely able-bodied and capable of earning a legal, legitimate living, and you were told that this person isn't even making an honest effort to look for work, how much of your hard-working tax dollars are worth supporting this person? Now increase that percentage 65, 70, and in some cases up to 85%. I took a silent anonymous poll over the last two years and asked virtually all of my fellow facilitation colleagues who check, view, and follow-up on the authenticity of their PT class job searches, and these are the percentages I received. On average, my colleagues, along with myself, felt that anywhere between 65-85% of our PTs' job searches are bogus, falsified, flat out untrue job searches. My personal investigations have led me to believe that in some classes up to 85% of the job searches were falsified. Think about it, taxpayers–you're busting your butt every day trying to make ends meet, stay above water, keep a roof over you and your family's heads and put food on the table, when a grown-ass, able-bodied and capable adult who you're supporting via your tax dollars isn't even making an honest effort in his/her job search. Every hardworking, tax-paying American should feel offended, insulted, and very much concerned about this type of support. Now, I'm not talking about the sincere PTs who are truly making an honest GAPS job search effort. I'm referring to those PTs who are making a mockery out of L.A. County's welfare-to-work system. The way the searches work is that the PTs fill out what we call employer contact sheets.

Each employer documentation sheet has 12 sections where PTs document company information such as date of application submittal, company name, full complete address, position applied for, person of hiring authority, action taken, planned follow-up. Now there are so many red-flags that pop up when we're reviewing their searches that we address each one accordingly. Without giving away all of our staff's trade secrets of our stellar investigative skills, oftentimes it's the lack of information the PT knows that gets them into so much trouble. Each facilitator operates differently on how we verify the authenticity of their searches; however, I'll share some of the common mistakes PTs make. I would say that at least 85% of all companies are utilizing online and in-store kiosk systems as means to pre-screen potential interview candidates. Therefore, the PTs submit either a print-out copy of their successfully completed online application, kiosk proof, business cards, and/or customer receipts. Now, our PTs are instructed to document searches in their career enhancement guide book, so that they always have copies/receipts of their daily activities. Next, they only spend between 30 minutes to an hour transferring their searches from their career guide books onto their employer contact sheets. This is where the cat and mouse game begins.

Let the games begin. Each day is a battle just to try and get a majority of our PTs to have all of their searches neatly, completely and accurately filled out with proofs. I'll methodically break down all the excuses they typically make for producing incomplete employer contacts. For having blank dates, the common excuses are: "Oh I forgot, I can't remember"; "You didn't say we have to fill in the dates"; "Why do the dates matter?" It's oftentimes like explaining to your five year-old why 8:00pm is their bedtime. You start off very nice and loving but after a while you say, "It's your bedtime because I'm the parent, I make the rules, and you follow them until you're grown and out of the house." The name and full complete address of the employers is chronically bad! They'll have the name of the company misspelled, incomplete address, wrong city, etc. One PT thought he could fool me with one of my favorite eatery spots. Not only did he flat out falsify the company information right in my face, but he couldn't even correctly pronounce the name of this particular restaurant. I played along as if I didn't know the correct information until I had enough of his blatant lies and checked him immediately. When I correctly pronounced the name of one of my favorite restaurants, his response was, "Yeah, that's it! That's the one!" I replied, "That's the one?"

The rest of the conversation went like this:

"Dude, you didn't go into that restaurant?"

"Yes I did! You think I didn't just because I couldn't pronounce the name?"

"No, I'm saying that because none of this information you put here is true to that particular restaurant. I eat there all the time. First of all, they don't have salesperson positions there. They have cashiers, hosts, bakery clerks, etc. But no positions called salespersons. Secondly, I know all three managers who work there and none of their names are José, so you just made up a manager's name, huh? Thirdly, if I were to call the company right now, I bet you they wouldn't even have your app nor resume on file." The PT was in absolute silence as he bowed his head in shame then suddenly tried to negotiate a make-up job lead. I informed him that due to this blatant falsified job lead, I'd have to call all of his remaining leads. He abruptly got up, left the room, failed to attend class the following day, and ended up self-dropping from the program.

In all honestly, if our PTs just focused on the job leads via Internet sites such as Cal-Jobs, Indeed.com, Career Builders, Monster, Linked In.com, etc., then they would have a plethora of choices to choose from. We provide them Internet access, along with some job development assistance. Unfortunately, our staff doesn't have the man-power to develop three to five job searches per PT every day along with teaching, paperwork, and other duties assigned. A large part of this job search approach is about EMPOWERMENT! What I've observed as a common trend in job search now is that a growing number of our PTs want what I call, "hocus pocus & abra cadabra" jobs, RIGHT NOW! As if our staff can just wave our "magic job wand" and grant them their ultimate job wish! And last time I checked, we don't have "genies in the bottle" for each of our PTs to receive three granted ideal job wishes!

One PT demanded that I complete all of his online applications because he was computer illiterate and wouldn't be able to complete the daily job search requirements of our program. I responded by instructing him to report to our job search lab room during our specified morning hours, and either one of my colleagues or myself would gladly walk him through one of his online applications. However, what we were not going to do was fill out every single job application on his behalf! That wasn't going to happen! It's about him having an independent and self-sufficient approach towards his job searches. He replied, "I caint get up that early in the morning, plus you guys are suppose to fill out all my applications." I had to remind him that we have a very busy daily schedule, and that we set aside specific lab time hours just for those PTs who need special individualized attention and assistance. Also, I told him that unfortunately, Barbara Eden's not on our payroll staff, where she could just blink up a once in a lifetime dream job for him.

It reminds me of the biblical parable paraphrased, "Give a man a fish and he'll eat for a day–teach him how to fish, and he'll eat for a lifetime." This PT wasn't willing to make the necessary effort and learn how to professionally "fish for jobs." Now back to the employer contact sheets. Many of our PTs also either forget the name of someone of hiring authority, or they leave off the phone numbers. One of our students allegedly filled out an application via the kiosk system, but she forgot to get both the phone number and manager's name. When I asked for a business card proof, her excuse was that no manager was available to give her a card. Hold up! Every place of business always has someone of hiring authority present, right? Even if it's the assistant manager, supervisor, or lead person, get their name, period! A large part of what we're teaching our PTs is to first of all overcome the fear/embarrassment of approaching persons of hiring authority–that's part of their job. Secondly, they want to directly introduce themselves to the movers/shakers of the company–people who are part of the interview process and who can make things happen regarding the overall decision making hiring process. This is one of the most effective face-to-face network marketing strategies. The application process "steps taken" section is generally incomplete, which tells me that little if any contact was actually done. Scheduled follow-up is typically a generic, "will follow-up." Follow-up when?

One guy allegedly applied for a sales clerk position at Starbucks. I said, "Dude, please! I'm a Star-buckie! I've been one for over 10 years. Every Starbucks restaurant I've ever patronized over these last 15 years doesn't have entry level counter position called 'Sales Clerks.' They don't exist!" So I asked him, "The persons serving the beverages/food?" He answered, "Yes!" confidently/emphatically.

I said, "Dude, the employees who serve the beverages/food at Starbucks are called 'baristas'!"

He responded by saying, "Oh yeah, that's right."

I replied by reminding him that he could be immediately dropped for falsifying job searches. So when I decided to call on six of his searches, all six were as phony as a four-dollar bill. Dude was flat out falsifying job leads! He lied about positions being available, putting down names of managers that didn't exist, locations of businesses. When I confronted him about these investigative falsified findings, he admitted guilt and asked to make up the six falsified searches, but I declined to accept any additional searches in lieu of his already submitted falsified ones. He then inquired about extra credit work. I reminded him that this wasn't his high school history class; this was about the professional integrity of his job search. Needless to say, he was dropped from the JSPC program as a result of falsifying job searches.

Therefore, the games that a significant percentage of our PTs play regarding job searches is truly mind-blowing! Now, it's humanly impossible to catch every PT's falsified searches because of the sheer number of searches they're required to produce each and every day. Traffic cops can't catch every moving violation out there, but when we get pulled over, don't we try and come up with an excuse for why we committed that moving violation? And hopefully get off with a warning and not receive a costly ticket? The same thing happens when we catch our PTs falsifying job searches. Here are some lame excuses PTs give us for not completing their daily job searches: 1. I had to baby-sit my niece/nephew; 2. My son/daughter was sick so I had to take care of them; 3. I had to take my mom/grandma to her medical appointment; 4. I lost all of my searches on the bus; 5. My car got impounded and all of my searches are in the car; 6. I couldn't reschedule my medical appointment; 7. I had to wait for the cable-man to come and install my cable; 8. My baby-mama dropped off my son/daughter to my house and I had to watch him; 9. I was sick, 10. I had severe P.M.S.; 11. I went out to eat last-night and left the searches in the restaurant;12. I had to go out of town, and I couldn't do 'em. One young lady tried to submit a napkin with handwritten company info on it and an advertisement cut-out straight from the newspaper. I told her that those were unacceptable proofs of job search. OK, first of all, you expect me to accept this napkin with handwritten company info? In the infamous words of Chad Ochocinco, "Child, please." "I'm not going to put a frickin' paper-towel napkin in your folder! How unprofessional and tacky would that be on my part to allow such ridiculous mess? Young lady, you are most definitely trippin!"

"I know, Jahi, I'm sorry. That's all I could get!"

"All you could get, huh? You didn't even try! I bet you, if I were to call the company and inquire if your application is even on file, I bet they'd say, 'No, it isn't!'" As she bowed her head in shame, I began to give her a serious pep talk about submitting genuine job searches. The conversation ended with her leaving my desk like a six year-old girl who had just been reprimanded by her first grade teacher. She was absent from class the next few days and subsequently dropped from JSPC. Another guy tried to show me a picture of an alleged job search on his camera phone, along with an old business card that looked like it was from 1985. It was so dirty, greasy, and wrinkled that I didn't even touch that hazardous item with my bare hands. I told him, "Dude look, you can't get program credit for pictures of companies on your camera phone, nor am I going to even consider accepting this 1985 business card that looks like you found in the dumpster! Ain't gonna happen, my man! You got to come better than this, dude!" As the stuttering/ mumbling began to crescendo, he tried to come up with a convincing comeback; however, he couldn't. I told him that I would have to follow-up on the rest of his job searches. That's when he suddenly became verbally defensive and frustration settled in on his face. He eventually confessed to not conducting authentic job searches. I responded by telling him that falsifying searches only hurts his future progress/success in the job market. He ended up being dropped due to excessive falsified submittal of job searches.

By our PTs falsifying job searches, it not only negatively affects their success in the job market, but it's also a blatant disrespect to you the taxpayer who's supporting a person who's defrauding you of your investment. Imagine one of your neighbors is out of work, and every family on your street decides to pitch in financially to help your fellow neighbor for the next nine months. Let's call him "Mr. Shady" just for example purposes. Now your entire block is going to pay their mortgage, bills, and other household expenses. In all, approximately 20 households are pitching in anywhere between $250-$300 dollars a month each. During the first couple of weeks, none of your neighbors are putting any pressure on Shady, just giving him plenty of motivation, job-development assistance, plenty of encouragement and support. All of a sudden, between months three and four, one of your neighbors walked by Mr. Shady's house at 10:00 am in the morning, while walking his dog on his day off, rings the door bell, only to find out that Shady is home watching "The Price Is Right" on television. And for the next couple of months, different neighbors run into him at the mall, movie theatres, Dodgers' baseball game, beach, etc. Now, he's not applying for any of those positions, just hanging out having fun! Wouldn't you feel just a little betrayed? Maybe even a little pissed off knowing that your hard-earned money is being wasted on a guy who's not even making an honest GAPS job search effort for employment? This is an able-bodied guy, who elects to chill, relax, and enjoy the money you guys are giving him, and he isn't even looking for work.

Sound familiar? This is a very common problem with a significant percentage of our PTs. Taxpayers are working first-, second-, or third-shift jobs trying to keep a roof over their families' heads, while many of our PTs elect to not to make an honest GAPS effort regarding their job searches. Think about it once again! Your tax dollars are contributing towards 400-600 dollars a month in state/federal funds per PT, Section 8 housing subsidy cost, significantly reduced child-care assistance, free mental health, substance abuse services, up to thousands of dollars of misdemeanor citations paid for, up to 90% or more of child-support arrears paid, weekly MTA bus passes, once a year clothing voucher, etc. And, once again, a significant percentage of our PTs have the audacity not to even make an honest effort in their daily job search? Excuse me! Major changes have to be made. Meanwhile, young 24 year-old Melinda is getting up at 4:30 am every day. She gets the kids up to get ready for day-care and school. Next, she gets on two different buses just to take them to their respective destinations for the day, and then Melinda takes three more buses just to get to work at a minimum-wage retail job that barely pays the bills. But Melinda is busting her ass trying to "do the right thing" and take care of herself and her children, while Mr. Shady over here is watching "The Price is Right." I have a lot more respect for Melinda than I do Ole Shady! At least she's an able-bodied, hard-working, tax-paying citizen who is earnestly trying to take care of her family and self. As taxpayers, who should we support–the Melinda's of the world, or the Mr. Shady's of the world? You make the call!

The majority of our PTs have very marketable skills/expertise where they can earn a legal/legitimate income. However, a combination of fear, lack of motivation, or lack of inspiration/desire to pursue their talented skill levels stops them. I've facilitated literally thousands upon thousands of PTs who are literally wasting their God-given abilities, learned skill-sets, and money-earning potential in various fields such as landscaping, cosmetology/barbering, automotive, construction, housekeeping, child/adult care provider, retail, and other service industries. The sky's the limit on what they could potentially achieve. One particular gentleman a few years ago was so skilled in landscaping that we all encouraged him to even apply for city/county tree-trimmer jobs. His two biggest obstacles were his multiple felony convictions and substance abuse. I encouraged him to slowly build his neighborhood clientele by going door-to-door and advertising via word-of-mouth marketing. Another young lady's cosmetology skills were off the charts. She wore one of the many hairstyles she knew how to do, and the entire class marveled at her artistic hairstylist skills. We encouraged her to personally visit every local beauty salon and speak with the management/hairstylist regarding employment opportunities. Her excuse for not following our advice was that she wanted to skip that very important part and just apply for her state license, which cost money. I reminded her that if she worked in a salon/beauty shop, or any company for that matter, at least part-time hours, she could start saving money towards her state license fees, all while still retaining a portion of her EBT benefits. Another barber dude had very impressive haircutting skills. He repeated JSPC class so many times that he could've taught the damn classes. Finally, one day after class, I sat down with him and we had a long discussion about his barbering talents. I basically told him that by habitually repeating JSPC, he was wasting valuable time and money, where he could be out there building his business. His response to me was, "Yeah, I know I gotta get out of being lazy and make it do what it do." I replied, "You think." So I encouraged him to vigorously pursue a career in the barbering business due to his skill level and overall enjoyment of cutting hair.

One of our other PTs could have been the Manny of Manny, Moe, and Jack of PEP Boys. This guy had excellent automotive skills. However, due to his felony convictions, and what I perceived as mental health challenges, he didn't want to pursue that career field. During one of our one-on-one search sessions, he was extraordinarily knowledgeable about every make/model of virtually every car on the road. He even told me that he knew how to do body work along with mechanical work. However, he needed to get state certified in order to work at most of the automotive companies. I suggested that he approach every automotive store and personally sell himself to the hiring manager. The construction guy had over 25 years on the field, but due to the overall economy/industry, business was slow. I encouraged him to speak with a Home Depot or Lowe's manager in the meantime and in-between time because, with his knowledge/expertise, he could be a very valuable asset to one of those companies. Our housekeeping young lady claimed there wasn't a house in America she couldn't spot clean and shine. My professional advice to her was "to put her money where her mouth was" and hit up every motel, hotel, and Molly Maid service. Someone's bound to give her a trial run to see how good her skills really are. For our child-care provider, I suggested the Girls and Boys Club of America, or YMCA/YWCA. Finally, I encouraged our adult-care provider to consult with In-Home Support Services of Los Angeles, and inquire about the high demand for adult senior/elder care employment opportunities.

But my stories aren't always as discouraging as these, as you'll see in the next chapter.

CHAPTER 17: *Diamonds in the Rough*

Over the years, we've had plenty of employment success stories that have enabled our PTs to totally remove themselves from the welfare rolls. Here are a few of my favorite "diamonds in the rough" stories. Back in 1997, there were four young women who entered one of my JSPC classes. This particular class comprised the typical barriers to employment such as illiteracy, felony convictions, substance abuse challenges, and mental health. Now, what struck me about these four ladies was that they all sat next to each other in the front row. During the first week of JSPC, where we covered our usual Pre-employment training workshop, all four ladies exuded high degrees of Positive Mental Attitude (P.M.A.). They enthusiastically participated in all the class activities, maintained perfect attendance and punctuality, and all four young women carried themselves with admirable professionalism.

Before the end of the first week, I met with all four of them after class and thanked them for their active participation in the workshops and for their overall invaluable contributions throughout the week. Boy, did I get one of the most heartfelt and inspiring surprises ever. All four had "baby daddy" drama. One of the guys was serving a long-term prison sentence, one of the other sperm donors was trying to avoid his parental responsibilities by living out of state, another guy was living out of the country due to immigration issues, and the other father was just a flat-out dead-beat dad. Each young lady briefly shared her compelling story one day after class during my lunch hour. The room atmosphere felt like we were on *Oprah* talking about single moms moving forward with their lives. I genuinely felt compassion for each young lady's personal situation. I had already reviewed their master applications and resumes and discovered that they were all very much employable. Each young lady used their children as inspiration, motivation, and determination to obtain employment. These young women were serious about making changes in their lives.

That very next day, on a Thursday, during the first week of JSPC, I was walking down the street to one of my favorite downtown Los Angeles

eateries during lunch hour when I noticed an employment opportunities hiring fair at one of the local hotels. On Friday the very next morning, I informed the entire class of 30-plus PTs to just go check out the
hotel's employment opportunities and see what departments they're
hiring for. Do you know how many of our PTs actually showed up that
day? Four! And guess which four? You guessed it, MY FOUR LADIES.
That following Monday morning, my four ladies couldn't wait to share
the exciting news that all four of them got hired in the following four
departments: housekeeping, restaurant and dining, personnel payroll,
and the fourth lady was hired as a reservations specialist. Each one
gave the class an emotional and inspirational testimony about not giving up and staying committed and fully invested in their job search.
There were very few dry eyes in the class as my four ladies shared their
stories, opened their hearts, and encouraged everyone to stay positive. All four ladies gave me thank-you hugs and reassured me that
they would stay in touch with us regarding future networking job
development employment opportunities within the hotel.

Later that year in 1997, another one of our "diamonds in the rough"
really impressed me. She had recently divorced her ex-husband as a
result of substance abuse, domestic violence, and stints of habitual
incarceration. The first few days in JSPC, she was sharp, insightful,
shared powerful job seeking tips, and overall maintained an incredible P.M.A. On the last day of the first week, we spoke after class about
her job/career goals. She inquired about obtaining my position as a
facilitator. So I gave her information about the experience, education,
and additional skills/abilities needed for this position. She had her AA
degree; however, she had no experience working with the adult welfare-to-work population. Nevertheless, her amazing spirit and positive mindset over-rode the lack of experience areas. Since she had a
striking resemblance to the very beautiful Chili from the legendary
female singing group TLC, we'll just call her "Chili." She began to tell
me a lot about her situation after class one day. Sadly, Chili had been
molested as a young girl, raped as a young woman, then fell victim to
an unhealthy marriage, where her ex-husband used her horrific child
molestation abuse as a means of controlling the marriage in an abusive
manner. At the time, Chili was going to therapy for all the emotional

stress she was dealing with in her personal life. But what gave her the ultimate motivation was her 12 year-old son. She mustered up every muscle in her body to take her son and leave that unhealthy marriage. Even her so-called devout Christian parents chastised her for wanting a divorce due to how it's generally frowned upon in the Christian faith.

One day Chili was sitting at her respective staff agency recruiter's desk when surprisingly, the recruiter asked her if she'd be interested in working for that staffing agency. It turned out that one of their other recruiters was relocating out of state. So with great enthusiasm, Chili responded to the recruiter with an emphatic YES! A few days later, the agency extended an interview invitation to her for the vacant recruiter position. Excited about the interview invite, Chili asked me to prep her on some interview questions. So I set up a one-on-one mock interview session with her the next day. We both covered all the basic/typical interview questions along with additional client matching, job development, and job placement preparatory questioning due to the type of work she was interviewing for. I also prepared her for a few role-playing questions just to make sure we covered all bases. Well, it all worked out because Chili got hired that same day by three managers. Filled with joy and overwhelming emotion, she told me that she broke down crying when they immediately offered her the position at the conclusion of the interview. When Chili came to class the very next day with the great news, the class gave her a warm congratulatory applause. She and I had a moment after class to complete the employment success form paperwork when she gave me the biggest hug and thanked me for all the support I'd given her. For the next several months, I referred various qualified PTs for temp-to-perm assignments to Chili and her staffing agency colleagues. Things were going well for awhile as our PTs were getting placed on job assignments, until one day she was pulled into the office by her site manager, and things changed…

After the long conversation with her boss, she called me on the phone to share the bad news.

"Hey Jahi, what's up? This is Chili."

"Hey Chili Sauce, what's up, girl?"

"I'm good. And you? Always a pleasure to hear your voice."

"Ditto, babe."

"Hey listen, my boss doesn't wanna work with your clients anymore."

"Uh oh! What happened?"

"One of them is suing us and the company we assigned her to for burning her bottom lip after pouring some hot water from the company water-bottle dispenser. Another girl filed a sexual harassment case against my boss just for saying, 'Congratulations Sweetheart' when she got placed on an assignment. The last one is scaring our employer by having her boyfriend and his neighborhood gangsta thugs pick her up from work every day." Chili went on to say how Ms. Lip Burn allegedly had to be rushed to the emergency room for third degree burns. However, she couldn't provide the employer nor us medical documentation supporting her claim. There were no witnesses that observed the alleged burn, nor could anyone detect any visual signs that she was indeed burned. When Ms. Lip Burn returned to the assigned worksite, she was instructed to file all medical proofs/ legal documents with the HR department. She couldn't provide medical proof of her alleged burn claim, and she was subsequently dismissed from completing the remainder assignment. Refusing to leave the worksite, she caused an unprofessional scene and was escorted out of the building by security. "Ms. Sexual Harassment is obviously just trying to get a big payday, but my boss isn't going to cave in and just settle out of court. Ms. Gangsta Love needs to tell her gangster boyfriend that it's highly unprofessional for her man to bring his boys up to her place of work, using profanity language, gangsta verbiage, and shaking the parking lot with loud bumping music. Needless to say, my boss doesn't want us placing anymore of your folks."

"Well, I can't blame him. I just appreciate the fact that you guys even hired all of the PTs that you did. Please tell your boss that on behalf of our program, we sincerely apologize for the severe lack of professionalism of our ghetto ignorant-ass PTs for blowing future PT assignment opportunities. And we'll never refer any of our Looney Tune characters to you guys again."

As Chili starts chuckling a bit, she said, "Jahi, I can't tell my boss that. You're crazy dude!"

"Tell your boss to tell Ms. Lip Burn to kiss his ass, Ms Sexual Harassment to slide down a stripper pole, and Ms. Gangsta Love to keep a good bail bondsmen on speed dial."

Laughing hysterically, "Jahi, you are a fool!"

"Chili, look girlfriend, if you don't find comedy in some of this ridiculous-ass PT behavior, you'll go crazy trying to sympathize with that nonsense."

"Yeah, I see your point. Dude, we should do Starbucks soon?"

"Let's do that, Chili. I'll hit cha up next week."

"OK, take care."

"You too, Chili." Chili and I have a nice brother and sister friendship, and to this day I can always call her up and talk about our welfare drama as well as successes. And she is without a doubt one of our biggest welfare-to-work success stories of all time. She ended up getting two promotions inside of a year with that staffing agency until they offered her an amazing transfer management position in Greensboro, North Carolina, back in 2000. Chili is doing very well with her new husband of five years and their beautiful family life in the North Carolina area. Much respect to the Chili family.

There are so many more feel-good PT success stories that we could literally do a three-part made-for-television mini-series, or make a couple of sequel motion pictures about their individual success stories. As a matter of fact, I'd venture to say that at least 15-20% of current eligibility workers and case managers for Los Angeles County DPSS are former welfare-to-work participants themselves, and I've had the honor and distinct privilege of working side-by-side with such distinguished colleagues.

CHAPTER 18: *Just A Few Thoughts*

Throughout the years, I've had so many "Ally McBeal" moments of thought while teaching class that I figured now is the perfect time to share with you folks some of those many thoughts that have crossed my mind over the years. As facilitators for what's undoubtedly the toughest welfare-to-work county in the nation, it's very therapeutic for all of us to find various ways to balance JSPC workshops with light-hearted humor, fun-filled exercises, and a healthy balance of entertaining activities. For me, it's those moments of inner thinking that enable me to maintain my calm and relaxed demeanor as I facilitate JSPC workshop presentations. Here are just a few of my many inner thoughts over the years:

1. What if there was an awards show for career lifetime welfare recipients? Man, there would be a lot of nominees up in here! After thanking God, who else would the winner thank?

2. No, the county doesn't have a retirement program for welfare recipients, fool!

3. And there's no 401k plan, no stock options/mutual funds, or Social Security benefits.

4. If you stay ready, you ain't gotta get ready. Thanks, Suga-Free... OK, I've said that in class before...

5. I know, if I slapped the taste out of your mouth, I'd go to jail for assault and get fired. However, what if I just slap the shit out of you?

6. Where's Dr. Phil when you need him?

7. This is some Jerry Springer drama up in here!

8. Oprah, help!

9. T.G.I.F. I say this EVERY FRIDAY!

10. Did I turn the stove off before I left the house? Darn it, I know I left the damn bathroom light on again. Southern CA Edison loves my absent-minded ass.

11. Man, if I got just a penny every time they swiped their EBT cards over the years, I'd be very wealthy by now! Gotta play Lotto tonight…

12. If you say our classes are dumb, then doesn't that make you even dumber for having to repeat this dumb class again? Dumbass!

13. You say you already know all this JSPC stuff and you really shouldn't be in this class for the third time this year. I could ask you, "Why aren't you employed yet?" But I'm sure you've heard that at least twice already this year.

14. I got hit up four times for money yesterday at Vons, Wells Fargo, Chevron, and Trader Joe's. I'm gonna go broke at this rate. I'll have to start telling beggars and panhandlers that I don't have any more money left on my EBT card.

15. Fellas, the next time you take a young lady out on a date, you may wanna check and make sure there's a "Now Accepting EBT" sign hanging on the building somewhere before you go running up the tab.

16. I know some of you ladies think that those cut-off Daisy Duke shorts, halter top exposed boobs, sandpaper-looking ashy legs; bunion-infected toes are sexy, but it's a turn-off! There are two spots in Los Angeles County where you'll fit in perfectly: Gage/Figueroa Street or Long Beach Blvd/Rosecrans Ave.

17. It's a beautiful day in the neighborhood. Would you be my…? Could you Be my…? Thanks, Mr. Rogers.

18. I am in no way, shape, form, or fashion a pimp, but I just wanna pimp-slap the hell out of you right now!

19. One thousand one. One thousand two.

20. Man, I love my job!

21. Why did I come to work today? Should've called in sick, damn it!

22. If I hear another person say "I'm a people person" during our mock interview sessions, I'm gonna vomit. It's "I embrace multi-cultural diversity," people. Come on, step up into the 21st century!

23. Is Jahi gonna have to choke a b_ _ _ _? Thanks, Wayne Brady.

24. Remember, there's no "I" in the word "team." And we can't spell the word "success" without "U." OK, I've said that a few times…

25. Guys, this is Job Club, not a nightclub. Stop trying to pick up chicks here.

26. Some may wonder what Kim Kardashian's talents are. It's pretty clear to me that she has very strong entrepreneurial talents at making millions… You go girl!

27. If your grill (teeth) is all jacked up, please take advantage of the county dental plan. As a matter of fact, go right after class and just do an emergency walk-in. If you're wondering whether or not they'll accept you without an appointment, just open your mouth and start talking. Before you'd be able to even finish a sentence, you'll be strapped onto the gurney and wheeled

away into the emergency room to have surgical dental procedure operation on that jacked up grill.

28. If they say, "Why? Why?" Tell 'em that its human nature. Why? Why? Do they do me this way? Thanks, Michael Jackson.

29. Hey, if your breath is atrociously barking, then we don't mind you bringing gum, mouthwash, mints, Listerine dissolves, etc. to class. Pop a few of those in your mouth before class, during break, and after class to ensure optimum and maximum fresh breath effectiveness.

30. This girl is wearing blue eye shadow, red blush, and black lipstick with matching pink hair with strands of blond streaks… Punk rocker? Nah. Didn't they die off in the 1990s? Halloween? No, it's still summer time. Then what the hell?

31. Why can't we be friends? Why can't we be friends? Why can't we be friends? Thanks, War.

32. Friends. How many of us have them? Friends. Ones we can depend on? Before we go any further, let's be friends. Thanks, Whodini.

33. Ladies, if your underarm pits are hairier than my underarm pits, then don't raise your hand in class. We'll have to work out some eye-contact signals/head-movement gestures as alternative means of getting my attention when you wanna ask a question.

34. Wanna get away? Thanks, Southwest Airlines.

35. I bet you Chad's gonna pick Ruby as his "Ultimate Catch." She caught his attention since the very first episode. Thanks, Chad Ochocinco.

36. Lord, please help us all today!

37. You're in your 30s still trying to gang-bang? Lay down your rags, stop gang-banging, and fill out a damn job application, you grown-ass man!

38. Does this look like Sesame Street? Is this a day-care? You can't bring your kids up in these classrooms and offices. They're running around using our desk items for play toys while you ignore their out-of-control, sugar-high behavior. Control your damn kids! Do you bring them out on the job searches too?

39. Two, four, six, eight, who do we appreciate? Welfare, welfare! Yea welfare!

40. Make my day. Thanks, Clint Eastwood.

41. Woosah! Thanks, Bad Boys II.

42. Dawg! Dawg!! I'm a grown-ass man! Thanks, Cedrick the Entertainer.

43. You down with EBT? Yeah, you know me. Who's down with EBT? OK, I took the hook from "OPP." Thanks, Naughty by Nature, by way Of the Jackson 5

44. She doesn't belong here. Very intelligent young lady.

45. He doesn't belong here–smart guy.

46. We do have diamonds in the rough that enter JSPC.

47. A penny for your thoughts, a nickel for your kiss, a dime if you tell me that you love me. I wonder what I'd get if I gave her a dollar?

48. Did you just pass gas in my face as your standing here asking me a question? Because our small area space smells really bad

right about now. Let's move over here away from the toxic fumes so I can breathe a little easier…

49. OK, I know everyone needs a job, but I don't blame a lot of these employers for not hiring a significant percentage of our PTs because if I were a business owner, how many of these folks would I hire? If the shoe was on the other foot…

50. Things that make you say, "Um." Thanks Arsenio Hall.

51. Last I heard, you still can't post bail with your EBT card.

52. However, I hear that you can swipe your EBT card in some strip clubs and grab a beer and a lap dance-compliments of hard-working taxpayers of course.

53. I'm rubber, you're glue. What bounces off me sticks to you. Thanks, childhood!

54. Dang it! Now I'm positive I left the damn bathroom light on again…

CHAPTER 19: *Empowerment*

We've had some memorable diamonds in the rough over the years that have made indelible impacts on our JSPC program, and in December of 1994, one of our sparkling diamonds made such that impact. She entered the first day of JSPC class nervous, unsure, and overall anxious about what to expect in Job Club. You see, she grew up in Mexico City, and she came here to the United States of America as a teenager with her mom in order to have a higher quality of life. Upon seeing how dedicated this young lady was to attendance, punctuality, quality submittal of assignments, job search, and obtaining employment, one of our retired Career Development Program Specialists encouraged this young lady diamond to apply for one of our Temporary Office Worker Positions (TOW). She did just that, and approximately four months later, she was hired on as one of our TOWs. Since that time she has been promoted to Career Development Program Specialist and has been an amazing co-facilitator, colleague, as well as good friend. During her TOW days, she would start out at 4:30 am. She would catch three buses while taking her three children to day-care/schools. By the time she got to work at 7:30 am, she produced both quality/professional administrative work. I first met Melissa in December of 1995. She introduced herself to me as a Job Search Assistant and that she would be assisting me with clerical/administrative paperwork in our JSPC classes. It didn't take long for me to notice her incredible work ethic. Her punctuality, attendance, interpersonal relationship abilities, and administrative skills were impeccable.

Melissa was always shy, quiet, reserved, and about-her-business at first. Therefore, I would intentionally say and do things to make her laugh/blush, just to get her to loosen/open up a bit and not be so tense. You see, in order to have longevity on the front-line in our profession/industry, there are a few crucial ingredients one must have in order to maintain one's sanity and ultimately mental, physical, emotional, and spiritual health. One must have comedy/humor, freedom of speech/expression amongst colleagues, music, and personality; faith/

spirituality just to name a few. We've had some of our colleagues in the past not last very long as a CDPS in large part because they didn't embrace this formula for longevity. Melissa was slowly but surely coming around to embracing all the main ingredients of longevity. However, what really catapulted her over the top was our division's San Jose GAIN Conference trip in November of 1996. The first night we arrived at our designated hotel for registration, dinner and–little did I expect–after-hours night life. Our division director surprised Melissa and me by assigning us the task of facilitating a workshop for 250 participants. I remember Melissa's facial expression looking like a deer in front of the high-beam lights. I responded to our director by asking him, "What's the theme/topic of the workshop?" He replied by telling us that it was up to us to come up with a theme/topic by the end of the next day and be ready to present the following morning. I assured him that we would come up with an exciting theme/topic. Melissa looked at me with disbelief

She asked me, "Jahi, how can we come up with an exciting workshop for 250 participants by Sunday morning?"

I said, "Melissa, don't worry. We will work on it all day/night if need be until we get it down pat. Plus, we get to come up with our own free-style theme/topic, which I absolutely love doing. We're gonna rock this workshop, girl. Don't worry. Trust me."

Well, that Friday evening after dinner, we went to visit my cousins who lived just five miles away from our hotel. We had a nice dinner/visit with them, then headed back to our respective hotel rooms and got plenty of rest that evening. The next morning was an early rise and shine. I called Melissa and told her that I had a few ideas for our workshop presentation. We discussed the details over breakfast, shopped for visual aid workshop items, headed back to the hotel, and practiced for a few hours until we felt confident to give our director a dry run-through.

The title of the workshop was "Fire 'Em Up!" The theme was about bringing fun game show activities to some of the JSPC curriculum. The game show we decided to showcase was "Family Feud." Melissa kept whiteboard score of the two teams' points battling it out over questions pertaining to applications, resumes, and interviews. I played the role of show host. The 45-minute workshop went exceptionally well. All 250 participants were enthusiastically participating in our "Fire 'Em Up" workshop. WE KILLED IT! WE ABSOLUTELY ROCKED DA HOUSE!! I dang near started break-dancing, cabbage-patching, and doing the electric slide I was feeling so good. At the conclusion of the workshop, so many of our colleague participants approached us with congratulatory compliments of how they absolutely loved our workshop. Melissa gave me the biggest hug of relief/gratitude. I reciprocated her thanks by reminding her, "That's how we do it, girl." We bring nothing but heat/fire to our workshops. It's the fabric of our professional DNA! As LACOE facilitators, our workshop presentation pedigree is second to none! With GIGANTIC smiles on our director's and other senior managers' faces, they all congratulated us on a very successful workshop. After leaving the hotel ballroom, we grabbed some lunch, and then rested up a few hours until dinner time. Later that evening, we all celebrated/partied like it was 1999 and we were the opening act for Prince and The Revolution. The rest of the night was like the old Vegas quote, "What happens here stays here."

I met another one of our diamonds in the rough in December of 2010, and he would reinforce to me that ALL of our PTs are able and capable of earning a legal/legitimate living. Big Brody served 29 years in Youth Authority (Y.A. incarceration), and adult prisons. More than half his life was confined in correctional facilities. On the first day of JSPC, I allow our PTs to verbally express themselves–to share their barriers to employment, short-term/long-term goals, and reasons why they're welfare recipients in order to transition them off the welfare rolls. When Brody began speaking about his 29 years of incarceration, you could hear a pin drop in the classroom. It was almost like one of our elder uncles sharing a powerful testimony of overcoming adversity via the power of our mindset, aka positive mental attitude (PMA). He spoke like he was Les Brown's national spokesperson. With eloquence, conviction, passion, and inspiration, Big Brody shut the room down with an unbelievable display of positive motivation. During the break time, I expressed my appreciation to Brody on how impressed I was with his inspirational testimony and that I'd welcome additional positive comments from him throughout the duration of JSPC. Well, for the entire first week of class, Brody arrived early each and every day, cemented a big championship smile on his face, enthusiastically participated in individual/group assignments/projects, and provided overall invaluable contributions to the daily JSPC experience.

At the beginning of week two, I had job-developed this staffing agency that specialized in placing uniquely skilled construction laborers for commercial contracting assignments in the city of Long Beach, CA. When I shared this information with Brody, his eyes lit up! He said, "Jahi, this would be perfect for me. I have both scaffolding and general commercial construction contracting experience." He followed up on that hot job lead that same day, received an interview the very next day by the recruitment manager, then received an assignment offer that same day. Brody was so happy because he had just relocated to the city of Long Beach, CA with his girlfriend, and the staffing agency was starting him off at $18 per hour salary, with the option of the company picking him up permanently after the successful completion of their 90-day probationary period. He came back to the office and gave me the biggest bear-hug embrace EVER. We were both jumping up and down like we had just won the Super Bowl and he was hoisting the Lombardi trophy. I was so happy for him. After the celebratory congrats and employment info completion of paperwork, I asked him if he would one day come back to our class as a guest motivational speaker and share his powerful testimonial story. He graciously agreed.

Just before New Year's Eve 2010, there was another PT who would be considered an all-star diamond in most circles. Kevin was raised primarily by his grandmother due to unfortunate parental challenges. He had just gotten released from Folsom State Prison after serving eight years on burglary charges and a total of 13 years overall. On the first day of JSPC, he shared with the class how his incarceration experience was not going to deter him from his career goal of becoming a successful author. During break-time, he showed me a copy of his published book and reassured me that his short term goal was to obtain a part-time job for the time being while focusing on his long-term goal as a published author. I purchased his book during the second week of class, and I couldn't put it down! This young man is a very talented author. And for the next 90 days, this young man's life began to gain progressive book momentum. From soaring sales of his book to radio show interviews and talks of television production deals, this young man's life-story is truly diamond-worthy. Kevin was a former gang member and made a lot of money via various illegal hustles. He served time in prison in a few of the most feared men's correctional facilities in northern California. He ran through cars, women, and hundreds of thousands of dollars. However, what gave him inspiration, motivation, and determination to turn his life around was his teenage son and the birth of his baby girl this past spring of 2011. I always tell our PTs who are either custodial and or non-custodial parents that their number one inspiration, motivation, and determination to obtain employment/earn a legal legitimate living should be their children. I mean, come on, really, what more motivation does a parent need than to look into their child's eyes and know they're responsible for taking care of them? How many times do we have to repeat this in orientation, JSPC, Fastrak, REP, and other DPSS programs in order to hit this point home? I've seen way too many custodial/non-custodial parents come through our program and express lack of desire and uninspired dispositions pertaining to earning a legal/legitimate living.

And finally, in the summer of 2007, I met a gentleman whose county badge read "Case Manager," but he meant much more to the district than that. Every day he walked the halls with a gleaming smile, courteous greetings, and overall incredible PMA. His personality was/ is simply magnetic! When he approached me about participating in some of the district activities, I immediately said YES. From the Black History Month recognitions, Hispanic/Mexican/Latino observances, and multi-cultural events to the holiday party celebrations and the Swoodie Awards; the Michael Jackson remembrance and "Puttin' on the Hits" as Morris Day and The Time, we had an absolute blast! The overall morale at the district was at an all-time high. His name was, simply, Capricorn. Does this name sound familiar? Well, this is the same Capricorn mentioned earlier. You see, four years ago, prior to 2007, Capricorn was sitting in one of our JSPC classes as a PT. He entered our program as one of those rare "diamonds in the rough" PTs who really shouldn't have been there. Nonetheless, he obtained employment at a bank while awaiting the status results of his Eligibility Worker application. Within a year of his completion of JSPC, Capricorn successfully completed the written/oral examinations and was subsequently hired and placed at the same district office where he once sat as a PT. What a true success story, huh? He is a daily walking inspiration that our PTs can obtain employment and achieve unbelievable success. If I were to take a rough guess percentage of how many of my fellow EWs/GSWs are former PTs, I would say easily 20%.

All of the aforementioned diamonds in the rough, along with other PTs who obtain employment, are great examples of how ALL of our PTs in Los Angeles County's JSPC program are capable of obtaining employment and to earn a legal legitimate income. This is why I feel our state of California should impose tougher lifetime limits on how long an adult can receive these welfare-to-work EBT benefits. The GR population should have a maximum lifetime of benefits for twelve months, with the option of receiving two three-month emergency extensions, contingent upon their being employed at least 32 hours per week. The custodial parents receiving EBT benefits would receive a maximum lifetime of benefits for eighteen months, with the option of receiving two three-month emergency extensions, also contingent upon them being employed at least 32 hours per week.

It's time for "tougher love." They can do it! This is doable! Do I feel that a significant percentage of our PTs could be diamonds in the rough? Yes, I do! Do I feel that a majority of them can improve their GAPS effort? Yes, I do! Finally, do I feel that 100% of each and every PT who enters our JSPC program can be successful in obtaining jobs/careers and earning a legal legitimate income? Yes, I do. They have unlimited potential to change the conditions of their lives, and now it's time for them to execute. I would further recommend that a modest portion of the tax dollars we would save on welfare recipients' benefits go toward funding Dog Bless USA for veterans, which provides our combat troops with housing, mental health/substance abuse treatment, physical rehabilitation therapy, and job training. Another portion of these annual savings would go towards funding youth between ages 18-24 for internship/externship employment training programs. The third and final portion of these annual savings would go into increasing state/federal felony rehabilitation paid training funding programs in collaboration with the Department of Rehabilitation.

It's time that we hold all of our capable and able-bodied welfare-to-work adults accountable for earning a legal legitimate living within the above-mentioned proposed time limits and be responsible for taking care of themselves and their families for the long-term future. They are capable of earning a legal, legitimate income! It's all about EMPOWERMENT. It's the POWER OF IT! THEY MUST WANT IT! THEY MUST BELIEVE IN IT! THEY MUST FIGHT FOR IT! THEY CAN DO IT! Nike Corporation reminded us all to "JUST DO IT."

ACKNOWLEDGEMENTS

First & foremost: My OMNIPOTENT heavenly Father and his divine holy trinity

The GREATEST Mother ever to traverse the planet earth, my Mom Jeanette

To Khalil, I am the PROUDEST father of the BEST son!

The man who takes a licking but keeps on ticking, my Dad Renaldo

The BEST younger brother an older brother could ever have, my Brother Bruce

The HOTTEST older sister a younger brother could ever have, my Sister Ingrid

R.I.P Lillian and Weaver Lee, Nana & Granddaddy

To all of my Uncles and Aunts

My entire collection of 1st 2nd and 3rd Cousins

To my first grade teacher for spanking my hand with a ruler when I misbehaved, Mrs. B

My first innocent crush and second grade monkey bars playmate, Princess Mary

Muhammad Ali, for being the Greatest of all time…

Bruce Lee for being my true Super-Hero

Speed Racer and Giant Robot before my daily walk to elementary school

Saturday morning ABC school house rock, I never was the same after Interjections

The SuperFriends and the Hall of Justice

Don Cornelius and the longest running music show EVER, Soul Train

To the BEST elementary school ever, Denker avenue in Gardena, CA

My favorite teacher at Denker avenue, Mr. Wren.

Peary middle school, for our dear & beloved Blanch Wilson, 1979, R.I.P.

Gardena Senior High for the Friday night football games, and for the cute girls-fond memories.

My Stepfather, for purchasing my very first car-It was a brown 1974 Mustang mach11

To ALL of my CLOSE family and friends…

California State University Fullerton for, FUN FOND, and MEMORABLE collegiate Moments.

George L. Williams of the Orange County Urban League for taking a chance on a young college graduate.

Barbara Dent Jiles for recruiting me from the Orange County Urban League over to the The Los Angeles Urban League, as an Employment Advisor.

Yvonne Haezart and Social Vocational Services for the REWARDING experience of Supervising developmentally challenged adults in vocational training.

Los Angeles County Office Of Education for 17 INCREDIBLE years-with such a STELLAR organization…

Los Angeles Department of Public Social Services, for the AMAZING services you provide…

And finally, this book would not have been completed without the OUTSTANDING work of: Photographer, Lumumba Dunduza, My entire Create Space Design Team; my three proof-readers, CD, Catherine, and Carey. You guys did a GREAT JOB!!!

May we ALL experience UNBELIEVABLE success during the remainder of our journey here on earth. GOD WILLING, and may GOD BLESS US ALL…

www.ingramcontent.com/pod-product-compliance
Lightning Source LLC
Chambersburg PA
CBHW070807100426
42742CB00012B/2275